David A. Stone

# Wired to...

MW00712581

# Clients

Get Inside Your Customers' Minds
for Success in Business Development

## New Edition

ACEC

AMERICAN COUNCIL OF ENGINEERING COMPANIES

American Council of Engineering Companies
1015 15th Street, NW, 8th Floor
Washington, DC 20005-2605
(202) 347-7474
(202) 898-0068
www.acec.org
ISBN: 978-0-910090-49-0

# Contents

# Dedication

*It may be safely trusted as proportionate and of good issues, so it be faithfully imparted, but God will not have his work made manifest by cowards.*

*Ralph Waldo Emerson*

This book is dedicated to the eradication of timidity and the birth of the bold.

# Part 1
# Getting Ready to Win

# Introduction

It has been almost 10 years since I first wrote *Wired: How to Crawl Inside Your Client's Mind for Success in Business Development*. In the intervening years a great deal has happened.

The A/E industry has grown and matured significantly. Whereas previously it was still a relative newcomer to the field of marketing and sales, now there is a wider understanding of the theory and process of winning clients and ongoing work. This, along with the increased presence of true marketing professionals in our industry, has provided an increased sophistication in the approaches, tools and products of the marketing and sales effort.

In the last 10 years, I have had significantly more experience with a broad variety of marketing and sales situations. As a consultant, I have been invited to participate in attempts to win projects of every size and description for every possible type of client. Some we have won handily. Others we have lost in a close contest. On still others, we have gone down in flames. Every one has taught me lessons about how to listen to hear what the client is saying and then go beyond the expected and predictable to communicate back to them value that they were not expecting.

During this period I also took a two-year hiatus from consulting to serve as vice president of marketing and sales at a large general contracting company. This experience helped me gain a better understanding of what it takes on a daily basis to put together the proposal documents, presentation slides, and props, to maintain proactive business development activities, and to coach the technical professionals and subject matter experts to also be master communicators.

3

Of course there has also been a huge increase in the amount and intensity of competition. As I write this, we are (hopefully) beginning the climb out of the worst economic downturn since the Great Depression of the 1930s. In my own city of Charlotte, N.C., an estimated 40 percent of the architects lost their jobs in the past year. Across the country, projects that might once have attracted 10 proposals are now seeing 40 and 50. Small and mid-sized firms that were previously able to count on a level of loyalty from the local community are now going head-to-head against mammoth national firms who are sweeping in to win anything they can that will help feed their hungry machine.

Back in the mid-1970s when I first started in this business, it was considered unethical to publish a business card as an advertisement. Advertising and promoting yourself in that manner was seen as unfair competition against your fellow professionals. In a little more than one generation we have traveled from that quaint position to a world of cutthroat, rip-out-your-heart-and-eat-it-for-breakfast competition.

Along the way, the bar for marketing and sales performance has been— and continues to be—raised considerably. This book is an attempt to help us all reach those new heights of sophistication and overcome that intense competition.

As you go through this book I'm going to be showing you some truly off-the-wall ideas for your proposals and presentations. Throughout, I want you to always remember that the objective is not to be cute or gimmicky. The objective is enormously serious and the approach is based on the art of communication. How do you get an idea that's in your head successfully transferred to another person's head so that they understand and are as excited about it as you are? I show you these techniques, not because they are unusual or novel but because they can more effectively communicate your ideas and your value.

Through all the new techniques and innovative methods to get your message across, there remains a core truth that must never change. Learn to be quiet and listen carefully to what it is your client is asking for. Sometimes they don't really know, but then it's your job to interpret and deliver results and value that go beyond their expectations.

Let's get started.

# 1

# The Art of Persuasion

The ultimate goal of marketing is to persuade. In business promotion or what might be called the 'brand building' phase, you want to persuade groups of decision makers that your firm should be at the top of their list when they begin to think about their projects. In sales, your objective is to persuade an individual or group that your firm, above all other competitors, is best suited to be awarded their project.

Often, this need to persuade includes a need for the prospective client to actually change his mind. He may already have someone else in mind to retain or he may believe that he doesn't need to retain anyone at all. Your job is to persuade him to change him mind and begin to believe that he must retain you.

If you were selling cars, this would be easy. Your client could simply take the product for a "test drive" and compare it with the competition. But that doesn't work in the delivery of professional services. Your client can't tell whether he likes your "product" or not until after you've finished the work. Nor, if he is unhappy with you, can he bring the work back for a refund.

## Some unusual vocabulary

Your clients know that they are taking a big risk, so your marketing challenge is to persuade them that their risk is minimal or non-existent. They have to be made to feel completely comfortable with their decisions.

Take note of the words we're using here. Words such as "feel," "comfortable," "like" and "happy" are not the words normally used when a design firm does marketing. More often, we count on measurable words like "experience," "education," and "track record."

The problem with the traditional approaches to persuasion in proposals and interviews is that we depend on massive amounts of data about the firm and long lists of experience to do our "persuading." While these might be useful as backup, they don't do a very good job in the "feelings" department. It's hard to get emotional about a list.

Every firm against which you compete has a list of projects that they've completed that is just as long as yours. Every project manager has a good education and strong experience. For every project you've successfully completed, they've got one, too. The lists essentially cancel each other out.

So why should a client hire *you*?

## Features versus benefits

Before we answer that question, let's look at a parallel, but very informative, situation outside the design professions.

I went shopping for a new suit not long ago. It was a reasonably mundane experience, but one that emphasized a point that top sales and marketing professionals have understood since the first caveman sold his friend a club.

As I examined suits in the first store, the salesman was eager to give me all the reasons I should buy my suit from him.

> *"Our suits are made from only the finest wool."*

> *"Our tailors are all trained in Europe!"*

> *"Our suits come with a one-year satisfaction guarantee."*

When I looked at suits in the second store, there was a subtle but very important difference in the way the salesman spoke.

> *"The top-quality wool in this suit means you won't have to worry about wrinkles when you're traveling."*

> *"The cut of the jacket, which our tailors learned in Europe, really complements your features."*

> *"If you're not satisfied, you can simply return the suit any time in the next year."*

Where the first salesman focused on the product I was about to buy and related all the features of the suit, the second salesman went an important step further.

*He turned the features of the suit into direct benefits to me.*

He understood that I didn't care so much what the suit was made of as I did what it would look like when hauled out of a suitcase after a cross-country flight. He knew that the tailors could have come from Mars as long as the suit made me look good. And he knew I wanted the convenience of returning the suit if I discovered it did not meet my expectations.

He also knew that I was there to buy a suit for myself. I was the center of attention in the relationship and he was happy to put me on a pedestal. Go back to the words of the first salesman and find the center of attention:

> *"Our suits . . ."*
>
> *"Our tailors . . ."*
>
> *"Our suits . . ."*

I was not mentioned once in his monologue. Now compare it with the words of the second salesman:

> *". . . you won't have to worry . . ."*
>
> *". . . when you're traveling."*
>
> *". . . compliments your features."*
>
> *"If you're not satisfied . . ."*
>
> *". . . you can simply . . ."*

He set me up as the main subject of his discussion and showed how the features of the suit would benefit me.

In spite of our civilized manners, in our hearts we all want to know "What's in it for me?" By shifting his sales pitch from the *features* of the suit to the *benefits* I would enjoy from it, the second salesman won my business.

## So what?

While you're hardly selling suits, your clients are very interested in the benefits your services can bring them. Unlike the art patrons of the Italian Renaissance, these clients are not hiring you to give you an opportunity to practice your craft. They retain your services because they want a specific outcome for themselves.

If you focus your sales effort on the features of your firm, the client is forced to translate those features into the benefits they seek. For example:

>  **Features statement:**
>
>  *"Our firm was founded in 1958."*

You *want* the client to think:

>  *"They've been in business for so long! They must have learned many lessons and won't make any mistakes on my project."*

But there's always a danger the client will *actually* think:

>  *"These guys are awfully old. I wonder when they last had a new idea?"*

Instead of leaving the client to infer benefits (or liabilities!) they might gain from your firm's age, why not tell them directly and ensure they know all the benefits?

>  **Direct benefit statement:**
>
>  *"More than half a century of accumulated 'lessons-learned' at our firm eliminates potential mistakes and brings many time- and money-saving ideas to your project."*

## More on features and benefits

Why might you want:

- A car with traction control?
- Wrinkle-free pants?
- A dishwasher with a 5-year warranty?
- Painless dentistry?

You don't buy them for those features. Instead, you buy them for the peace of mind when driving in slippery conditions, the freedom from ironing while travelling, the assurance of reliability and the anxiety-free experience of keeping your teeth healthy.

Not long ago I was working to help a large construction company fine-tune its marketing message. We spent some time brainstorming about features that the company had to offer its clients. Here are some of the items we came up with:

- Safety record
- Awards
- Track record
- Volume of work
- Great people
- Systems and procedures
- Community involvement

We then went through an exercise to translate each of these features into key benefits that will accrue directly to their clients.

The company's safety record becomes the clients'

- Lower insurance costs
- Reduced project costs
- Avoidance of bad PR
- Happy workers
- Peace of mind

The company's awards become the clients'

- Prestige and recognition
- Comfort
- Reduced risk

The company's track record becomes the clients'

- Reduced risk
- Increased likelihood of on time/budget
- Reduced time demands
- Better decision-making

The company's volume of work becomes the clients'

- Reduced costs through buying power
- Increased speed through leverage on subcontractors

The company's great people become the clients'

- Pampered attention
- Ease of communication
- Extended network
- Access to important information

The company's systems and procedures become the clients'

- Trust
- Reduced risk
- Comfort
- Ability to focus on other priorities

The company's community involvement becomes the clients'

- Extended network
- Prestige
- Link to additional opportunities

You get the point. Your customers and prospects don't care about the features of your company—they care about the benefits that will accrue to them. So focus on the benefits and leave the discussion of features to your came-in-second competitor.

## And now back to persuasion

There is another, perhaps more important reason to focus on benefits rather than features. It gets back to our discussion about persuasion and has to do with everyone's favorite subject—which is, of course, ourselves.

Our constant focus on "What's in it for me?" tells the smart salesperson (and business developer) to focus on the customer, not the service being sold. In the previous example where the firm makes the features statement, "Our firm was founded in 1958," the cynical or preoccupied client may respond simply and rightly, "So what? What is it about the fact that your firm began so long ago that could possibly be of interest or benefit to me?"

The client did not set out to hire a firm of a particular age. They set out to find a firm that could complete their project on time and within budget, give them extraordinary value for the fees they pay, and ensure a long-lasting, high-quality facility investment. If that firm was founded two weeks ago and has a way to produce those outcomes, the client will hire them.

The fact that your firm has been around for more than half a century is irrelevant. "So what?" says the client. What *is* relevant are the lessons you've learned that will bring them a solution more quickly, the procedures you've developed that will ensure high quality on their project, and the network you've established that will smooth the way for an early completion for their project.

## Avoiding the "Trite Trap"

Having been sentenced to read hundreds of proposals and sit through countless presentations over the last two decades, I have concluded that much of what is presented as valuable content in design firm proposals and presentations is in fact, trite and meaningless rubbish.

Sound harsh? To add some science to this otherwise gut-level conclusion, I developed what I call the "Trite Test" that can be applied to any communication, written, verbal, or electronic that you send to a prospective client in hopes that you'll be hired. Here's how it works:

Since the ultimate objective of all marketing is always differentiation, it's reasonable that any statement you make in a marketing context should work to distinguish you from the other guy. To apply the Trite Test ask the following question:

> *"Could I imagine one of my competitors, in an effort to differentiate from me, saying the opposite of what I've just said?"*

Let's try it on a tired, worn-out statement used in most proposal cover letters.

> *"Acme Engineers is pleased to have the opportunity to submit this proposal."*

Apply the Trite Test and see if you can imagine someone writing:

> *"We're really annoyed at having to prepare and submit this proposal."*

Of course not! The fact that you were pleased to submit is self-evident. If you had not been pleased you wouldn't have bothered. So it's a corny statement that adds nothing to the value of your submission.

When you realize that every cover letter of every proposal begins with that sentence (or some variation), it becomes even more clichéd. Worse, instead of setting you apart, it reinforces the perception that your firm is just like everyone else who has submitted.

Here are a few more hackneyed statements that I see regularly in one form or another in marketing copy.

*"We are uniquely qualified for this project."*

While it might be true, the statement by itself proves nothing. Instead of using this stale claim, get specific with examples of your unique qualifications:

*"Our unique scheduling process will ensure the smooth operation of the rest of your facility during construction."*

*"We will meet your schedule and budget."*

Imagine buying a new car and having the salesman tell you that *"you can count on it to start every morning"!* Reliability like that grew to be expected long ago and we've moved on to much higher expectations. Likewise, clients today fully expect that you will meet schedule and budget – that's merely the price to get in the door. Now you have to show what you're going to do that's above and beyond the minimum requirement.

*"We will exceed your expectations."*

A nice step up from the previous example but still a generic cliché. How can you exceed my expectations before you find out what they are? Instead of making this trite statement, why not tell the client that your process includes a meeting specifically designed to identify and quantify their project expectations. Your team then establishes goals and procedures to go beyond those goals by a measurable 10 percent.

Clichés do nothing to persuade a prospective client to choose your firm over another. In fact, they strongly reinforce the impression that yours is just like all the others.

Ask a trusted client if you can borrow some copies of old proposals they have received from other companies. Review them and see for yourself just how much they sound like yours. Then purge all the tired, commonplace and unoriginal statements from your marketing and sales literature so you can begin to stand apart from the crowd.

# You're selling to humans, not machines

Now, let's get back to that important question: Why should a client hire *you?*

They will hire you because you realize that your client is a human be-ing, not a computer. If you were trying to sell your services to a com-puter, you would analyze your capabilities on a spreadsheet and the winning firm would quickly become obvious.

Human beings, however, respond only marginally to spreadsheets and more positively to enthusiastic, convincing and, yes, logical arguments.

In order to persuade successfully, start by learning how the "persuadee" thinks. Crawl inside their heads, find out what's important to them and identify the benefits they're seeking. Once you understand the view from your client's side of the desk, tell them how the direct ben-efits they'll derive from working with you will be the answer to their every prayer. And while you're at it, leave the trite statements to your competition.

# 2

# The Three-Stage Selection Process

How do you buy stuff?

If you're buying a new car, you walk around it, sit inside it, sniff its new-car aroma and take it for a test drive. If you're buying a shirt or a dress, you take it into the fitting room, try it on and check yourself out in the mirror. If you need a new cordless drill, you see how the various models feel in your hand and how they sound, and you might even drill a test hole or two.

Then, if you take the drill, the dress, or the car home and then discover that it doesn't fit or perform the way you expected, you return it: for a refund, a replacement or a warranty claim.

But what if you're shopping for a vacation? A tax-return service? A college for your kids? Or, heaven forbid, an engineering, architecture or environmental firm? How do you make up your mind about what to buy and whom to buy from in those situations?

There are two kinds of things you buy: You buy "stuff," which you see, touch and try out before you decide to purchase. And you buy services, which can't possibly be tested until the actual delivery of the service. And just to add to your stress, services can't be returned after delivery if you're not satisfied. In fact, what you buy is actually quite invisible.

## Searching for the intangibles

Your clients have long recognized that what they buy from you falls into the second category. They understand that they aren't buying the bricks and mortar of a building, the pumps and pipes of a treatment plant or the asphalt of a new highway. They are buying your creativity, your responsiveness, your resourcefulness and your ability to organize and manage a team.

If you're in a building as you're reading this, stop for a moment and look around. There was likely an architect, an engineer and a contractor involved in the construction of the building, so look to see if the project manager returned phone calls in a timely manner. While you're at it, see if the superintendent for the general contractor was a pain in the neck during meetings.

Of course you can't see any of this by looking at the finished building. These intangibles do not physically exist, yet they were a major factor in your client's decision-making in the first place. They are the very things on which most consultant selection decisions are made.

## How do your clients make their hiring decisions?

Think about how clients (and you and I, for that matter) make decisions. We love to believe that their conclusions are reached in a rational, logical fashion. They take all the consultants, line them up in some manner, and rationally, logically evaluate them until the firm that is "most qualified" somehow rises to the top of the heap.

To be fair, logic does play a limited role. Clients do, in fact, conduct a rational evaluation. They compare costs and evaluate technical capability. The truly incompetent are quickly weeded out and the moderately qualified are also pretty easy to identify and eliminate. But once your client has satisfied himself that he has identified the firms that are fully qualified to do the work, what then? How does the client determine who is "most" qualified when everybody is "fully" qualified?

That's when the gooey stuff enters the picture and the client falls back on other, less tangible criteria. Having satisfied themselves that the firms included on the short list can all correctly execute the project at a reasonable cost, they begin to look for those intangibles. Political issues and preferences come into play. Decision makers ask, "What's in it for me?"

They want to know, "Would I be politically wise to hire your firm?" "Would I be taking any risks by selecting you, because my boss likes someone else?" "You might be the most qualified but what will you do to make me look good?" "Why should I go to the effort of the fight it will take to convince Councilman Jones to go with you instead of the other firm?"

Seeking answers to questions such as these, clients have cleverly devised a three-step selection process that ensures that all their concerns are addressed and they have picked the firm that is most suited to that project in that place at that time—which may or may not always be the firm that is most qualified.

The problem is that we don't always recognize the purpose—and the opportunity—of the three-step selection process.

## What is the three-step selection process?

On the way to winning any given project, you're likely to find yourself involved in any or all of the following:

- You become aware of the client.
- First introductions are made.
- You make a formal sales call to introduce the client to your firm.
- You spend time getting to know the client and you may meet them at, or invite them to participate in, various social events.
- The clients asks you to submit a Statement of Qualifications (SOQ) .
- The clients asks you to submit a proposal in response to a specific project.
- You make the client's short list and participate in an interview/presentation.
- You are selected for a project.

You don't go through this prolonged dance when you're buying a car, so why do it now?

The reason is that your client is shopping for intangibles. They are buyers in search of the right consultant. But since they can't take the consultants for a test drive, they go through the three-stage selection process instead. Although the preceding list contains eight items, they can be "chunked" into three primary categories or stages:

1.  Business development, in which the client gets to know you
2.  Written proposal document, in which the client determines your technical qualifications for the project
3.  In-person interview or presentation, in which the client gets to see how you behave and respond under fire

At each of these stages the client will ask a different set of questions. There are very different things that they want to obtain and determine at each stage. You, on the other hand, tend not to cooperate with this agenda. Let's look at how you may typically handle each stage.

Stage 1

> You're in that first introductory meeting with the client and you pull out your brochure and start talking about your qualifications. Later, on the golf course, you talk more about your qualifications.

Stage 2

> You are invited to submit a proposal and you spend your entire 20 allocated pages describing your qualifications.

Stage 3

> You're standing in front of the client in the interview and you review your qualifications.

Three different times, in three different venues, you have answered the same question—but it may not necessarily be the question that your client wanted answered at each step. Let's talk about this a little longer because this is a really fundamental point in learning to be more responsive to your clients.

## Stage 1

The real purpose of the first stage is that the client wants to know, "Where do you fit into my grand scheme of things?" Through a brand- and relationship-building effort, they are asking, "Are you a big firm that can take care of all kinds of different stuff for me? Are you a small, niche capability firm that has specialized expertise and can take care of this particular problem? What pigeonhole should I stick you in in my world? Where would you fit?

They are also trying to find out what you are like as individuals and how you answer questions such as, "Can you hold a conversation? Can you demonstrate that you're the least bit interested in me? Who else do you know and how else might you be able to help me? Are you someone I can trust?"

At this stage there is no project. The client isn't hiring anyone for anything. They are simply getting to know you and seeing where you fit into their world. While general qualifications are part of the answer in this stage, they are by no means the only answer.

## Stage 2

Now there is a project. At this point the client says, "I'm looking to hire someone because I need expertise to help me with this project."

In stage 2 the client asks for written documentation. They might ask for a statement of qualifications, they might ask for a written proposal, or they might separate these and ask for both in sequence.

The questions they are asking at this point are, "What are your specific qualifications, credentials and experience that are applicable and of consequence to this particular project?" "Are you capable of executing the technical portions of this project for me?" "How might you approach solving the technical challenges that this project poses?"

What the client is doing here is sorting out the firms and individuals who are capable of and suitable for this project from those who are not. They want these submissions in writing because that lets them quantitatively compare apples with apples, after which they will then be able to create a short list of qualified firms: "Of the 15 firms that submitted, 11 do not appear to be suitable for this project." (But that doesn't mean they aren't suitable for a different project down the road.)

At the end of stage 2, the client has narrowed the list to four firms. They have carefully reviewed all the qualifications—education, experience, approach—and satisfied themselves that each of the four firms has the technical capability to do this job. The bridge or building or airport will be designed and built, it will work and it won't fall down. Now their challenge is to sort through those remaining four.

## Stage 3

Your client now enters a totally different phase of the selection process. They have a completely different set of questions they need answered, questions that can't be answered in a written format or on the golf course.

Their most important questions are, "How do you handle stress?" and
"What can I expect from you on this project?" The reason they now want
you there in person, in contrast to answering questions in writing, is that
they want to see how you are as a communicator and how you respond
on the spot. Can you stand in front of a room and be understood? How do
you handle it when they throw you a curve ball, because on this project
you're going to have curves thrown at you? How will you handle that?
Do you get flustered? Are you smooth? Do you answer honestly? What's
it actually like to be in the same room with you? Since you and they are
going to be spending the next six months up close and personal together
working on this project, can they stand to be with you? Are you the kind
of person that they'd actually like to work with?

As you can see, at each stage the client has very different questions they want
answered. While your qualifications are the answer to some of those questions, they certainly are not the answer to all of them. In fact, submitting a
full qualifications package (as opposed to a targeted excerpt) just might prove
that you *don't* have the right answer to one or more of the questions.

## Helping your client with their questions

In contrast, at each stage many firms simply give the client the same answers over and over again. They don't pick up on the fact that the client
isn't looking for the same answer at every stage. They want a different set
of answers, but some firms either missed the point or weren't paying attention to what the client were saying to them.

To be sure, clients are as bad at writing RFPs as many firms are at writing
proposals. So it's up to you to help your client. Many clients aren't consciously aware of the fact that they are seeking answers to different questions. Subconsciously they probably know it, but you have to help them
along by being one step ahead. You need to think, "Here's why the client
is interviewing us, so let's make sure they get the answers to those questions. Here's why they are asking for a written submittal, so let's be sure
they get the answers to those questions."

Our industry has become somewhat programmed in our responses, so
it's necessary for us to become deprogrammed. We're all guilty—we've all
learned a certain way. We're most comfortable talking about our firm, our
history, our experience and qualifications. And thus, we forget to listen
and ask the right questions, and then we forget to answer the right questions at the right time.

# 3

# Business Development

Let's go back and spend a little more time examining something we talked about in the last chapter.

We asked the question, "How do you buy stuff?" More specifically, we asked how our clients decide whom to retain when they are buying design services.

## No-risk shopping

Your clients buy stuff all the time. They take their children to the store to buy new shoes. They shop for clothing, furniture, tools, food, recreational equipment and school supplies. And when they choose to "buy" your services, it's just another item in a long list of "stuff" that they purchase every day. But the way that your client decides about and then buys design services is fundamentally different from the way they buy all the other things—a car, five pounds of flour, a pair of shoes or a power drill.

When you buy a pair of shoes, a new dress, a car or any other material thing you go to the store and then you get to try it out. You try it on, you test it, you determine if it works properly and whether or not it will be appropriate for the situation you have in mind. If you're buying a car, you take it for a test drive to see how it performs.

All this you get to do *before* you part with your money. You get to spend all the time you want in the store, trying clothes on, looking in the mirror, asking opinions and then trying something else. Then, if you ultimately determine that "No, this isn't right for me," you get to walk away and it hasn't cost you a nickel.

However, if you try on the shirt and decide that it does fit, it looks good on you and suits your needs, then and only then must you give them your money. That's a great feature of buying a car or a pair of shoes. It costs nothing to try it out.

Then let's say you get the pair of shoes home and realize that they don't fit quite right or you find a flaw that you hadn't noticed before. What do you do then? You take it back. And the store either gives you a re-placement or they give you your money back or they repair it under warranty. Your risk is very, very low. You have a built-in safety net.

# High-risk shopping

But now let's look at something very different. Let's say you're shop-ping for a vacation for your family. You're looking for a nice resort for a relaxing and fun-filled week. How do you try out this resort ahead of time and prove to yourself that it is going to be a great vacation?

It can't be done!

You can check online or read brochures from the travel agent and see that the place looked great on the day they took the pictures. You can talk to other people who have been there and most of them will prob-ably say that they had a wonderful time. (Who's going to admit to hav-ing spent money on a terrible vacation?) And you can talk to the sales staff at the resort and they'll all tell you how wonderful it's going to be.

Every one of these pieces of evidence is an indicator that your vacation is likely to be good. But none of them is proof.

So, based on the brochures, the testimonials and the sales pitch, you book the resort and buy the plane tickets . . . and proceed to have the worst vacation you've ever experienced. It rains for the entire week, the service is mediocre and the food is just barely edible. Where do you go to get your money back?

You can't! You're stuck. You can complain and they'll probably apologize. They might even offer you a discount for the next time you go to their resort. But beyond that, there is no recourse. There is no safety net.

This applies equally when your client goes on a vacation, sends her kids to college, has her tax return completed or buys design or consulting services.

Faced with this dilemma, how do your clients determine that "Yes, this is the perfect firm for me and my project?" They can't try you out ahead of time. They can ask for indicators, which come in the form of past projects, résumés and client testimonials. But these are only indicators, not proof that things will go well for this client on this project.

Then, after they've decided to hire you and it goes bad and they can't get their money back, what can they do? Yes, they can hire lawyers, but then everybody loses even more.

This is a high-risk decision. There's a lot at stake and a lot of intangibles to cloud-up the decision-making process.

## The vital role of business development

This is precisely where business development comes in.

Before we go any further, let's give it a definition:

> **business development,** *n.* The proactive cultivation of a personal, trust-based relationship between individuals who have interest and motivation to do business together.

Part of this definition deserves repeating: a personal, trust-based relationship between two individuals. You've been taught since your first day on the job in this business that relationships are vital for success. But it's likely that no one ever explained why they are so important.

Let's think about that client facing that high-risk decision: Make a good decision, hire the right firm and you, the client, look like a hero. But make the wrong decision, hire a firm that lets the project get out of control and go bad, and it's all going to be your fault. Who can live with that kind of stress?

Her selection boils down to whether or not she has trust and confidence in the company and the individuals who will be working with her to provide the service she's looking for. She's about to take a leap of faith – she's going to sign on the line based on a promise that everything will be okay.

So your client looks for a way to make the intangibles a little more concrete. She does it through a relationship with you. She's going to evaluate the quality of her relationship with you. Does she know you? Has she seen you in action in other situations? Has she seen how you make decisions? How you react under stress? Has she had a chance to evaluate your morals and ethics? Can she look you in the eye and know that you're going to be as good as your word?

This personal, one-to-one relationship is vital because at the end of the day, the only thing she has to go on is when you look her in the eye, shake her hand and say, "I'm going to look after you," and she is able to say, "Because I know you, I believe you. I trust you. I've got confidence that you will look after me."

That confidence does not come from a brochure. And it doesn't come from a written proposal. It comes from a trust-based relationship between two individuals. It comes because that client knows and trusts, at a personal level, the individual who looks her in the eye and makes that promise. Now, after she has signed the document and made that commitment, she can go home and go to sleep at night knowing, in the pit of her stomach, that things are going to be just fine.

The lesson here is that connecting with your clients on the technical level in a proposal or presentation isn't nearly enough. If you haven't connected with them on a personal and emotional level through your business development activities, there isn't a chance that you're going to win that job.

## How does business development work?

There is a great little book written some time ago titled, *All I Really Need to Know I Learned in Kindergarten.* Author Robert Fulghum made the case that life is about getting along with others and playing well together in the sandbox, all of which we learned by the age of five. We could easily adapt the title of that wisdom-filled book to *All I Really Need to Know— About Business Development—I Learned in Kindergarten"* because the secrets to success in business development are very similar to the secrets to success in life in general.

In a one-to-one business connection, both people know that success in the world of design and consulting is based on solid, trust-based relationships. The building of those relationships is the goal of business development. The simple rules of business development—of relationship building—ensure that the relationship between two business colleagues is based on the trust that is necessary for your client to comfortably and confidently prefer your firm over the others that are equally qualified.

Let's look at some fundamentals of business development that, when consistently practiced, will put you in the position of "preferred provider" long before the selection process for a particular project ever begins.

# Everybody has the same favorite subject

Everyone in the world has the same favorite subject—themselves. Perhaps it's genetic self-preservation or maybe it's just human nature, but all of us are self-centered to one degree or another. At some point we all want to know "What's in it for me?"

If you have any doubt about this notion, try this simple experiment. The next time you're at a social gathering—a neighborhood party or a business reception will do—walk up to someone you don't know, introduce yourself, and then begin talking about yourself. Tell them about your job, your family, last summer's vacation, your hobbies, your favorite sports teams and your pet turtle, Ralph. As you're talking about yourself, keep track of the time and see how long it takes until your new "friend" finds an excuse to end the conversation and move on to someone more interesting than you.

Then move on to part two of the experiment. Find another person you don't know, introduce yourself and begin asking them questions about themselves. Ask about their job, what they enjoy most about it, what they find the most challenging. Ask where they went to college and how their school's football or basketball team is doing. Ask how they like to spend their leisure time. With each of these questions, be very sincere, pay close attention and ask follow-up questions whenever you can. Keep an eye on how long this conversation goes on. You will invariably find that it lasts much longer than the first and that you may have made a new friend. Why? Because you spent the whole time talking about his or her favorite subject. You shifted the conversation to put them at the center of the universe.

Where is the center of the universe? It's right there where you happen to be right now, just like it is with everyone. The first and most important rule of business development etiquette is to put your client at the center of the universe and focus on his or her favorite subject.

## Every relationship is important

One of the worst things you can do is to let the other person know that the only reason you're interested in having a relationship with them is for the work that might come from it. Far too many design and environmental professionals who are just getting started in business development open the relationship by asking, "Do you have any projects coming up?" You might as well say, "I have no interest in you except to the extent that you might be a source of revenue for my company." The relationship is first. Any work that comes from it is a bonus. But make no mistake, work will come from strong, trust-based relationships if you treat your friends well. They will want to treat you well too and part of that good treatment involves helping your company prosper.

Not all your relationships will be direct sources of work. Many of your friends will simply be great sources of information, provide connections to other important relationships or give you advice and encouragement when you need it. But all your relationships are important and they all deserve to be treated with care, respect and gratitude.

## Shut up and listen

You were born with two ears, two eyes and one mouth and, as your mother said, you're intended to use them in that proportion. There is far too much valuable information that we miss when we're talking. Let the other person talk. When you talk, use your time to ask questions— lots of probing questions that not only get you more information, but that show you're genuinely interested. If you can't wait for the other person to finish speaking so that you can get your two cents in, you're missing a huge opportunity to build a high-quality relationship and learn some valuable information. So listen, observe and keep quiet.

## Pay attention

I was recently talking to the business development rep of a design firm who was complaining that he'd spent the previous evening at a City Council meeting and there wasn't a single thing covered in the meeting that had anything to do with his firm. He considered the night a complete waste of time. I pointed out to him that, while the meeting may not have discussed topics that applied to him directly right now, there were surely discussions and decisions that affected other people that he knows. Sure enough, within the next week he reported back that he had been able to pass on a piece of information to another client that proved very important and for which his client was very grateful.

## Watch trends

Your clients are down in the trenches, focusing on their business or agency. You, in contrast, have the luxury of seeing their operation along with many others like it. That gives you the ability to spot trends as they emerge and long before your clients may become aware of them. Be on the watch for trends and market or industry developments that would be of interest to your clients and pass them along. How do you spot trends? Start with the previous bit of advice to "pay attention." Watch out for news or developments that you haven't seen before. If you've seen something that seems new and important, be on the lookout for a recurrence of it or for another, similar news item. If you see it a third time, it's "officially" a trend and worth passing on to clients and colleagues who may be interested or affected.

## Let your warts show

None of us particularly like being caught at our less-than-best. But letting your clients and colleagues see the less perfect side of you shows you to be real. It's especially important when you mess up (and who doesn't mess up periodically?) to 'fess up and admit your mistake. This gives you a credibility that you can never achieve by always claiming to be right or infallible. If they see that you're honest as you deal with mistakes, they will assume that you are honest in all your dealings. We all make mistakes. It's what you do after the mistake that separates the good from the great.

## Be memorable

In our business relationships we want to be "front-of-the-mind" with our clients, colleagues and associates. We want them to think of us first when an opportunity arises, an important piece of news breaks or a key introduction needs to be made. You can make yourself memorable by being a valued and frequent member of their network. Keep them in the front of your mind. If your trip to a meeting takes you past a client's office, stop in just to say "Hello." Keep birthdays and holidays in mind and be sure to send a note or a card. Pick up the phone regularly and inquire how they're doing. Treat them as you like to be treated.

### Send notes

In this world of voice mail, email and instant messaging, there is something wonderfully warm and sincere about the handwritten note. When was the last time you got one? If you've received one in the past year, I bet you not only remember it, you've likely kept it too. These special communications are so rare today that they stand out among all our other correspondence. All emails, on the other hand, look the same and they're far too easy to delete after a quick scan, forever to be forgotten.

Try this instead. Carry with you a supply of small blank note cards, each one already inserted in a pre-stamped envelope. After you've visited with a client, a prospect or a colleague, and before you drive off to the next meeting, take two minutes and handwrite a short note, thanking them for their time and expressing how much you appreciate the relationship. Write the address on the front and drop it into the nearest mailbox. They will receive the note the next day and it will be kept and remembered for months to come.

### Give back

Too often we go to clients, prospects or associates asking for something. Whether it's a job, a lead, an introduction or valuable information, we want something from them. But what have you done for them or given to them recently? Before you can ask, you have to give. Even if it's your time, your knowledge or your friendship, you are obliged to give before you get. It's another one of those things we learned in kindergarten!

### Say "Thank you"

You can never say "Thank you" too many times. Express your gratitude for the friendships you enjoy, the assistance and guidance you are given, the revenue you depend on and the sustainability of your business because of the people with whom you work. Your mother was right: don't forget to say "Thank you."

Why is business development so important in the A/E world? It's because competence, technical expertise and experience are just ante into the game. Many clients aren't even capable of evaluating expertise and those that are get it out of the way quickly. But they can tell if they like you and if you return calls on time.

## Hunters and gatherers

Different firms handle business development in different ways.

Some ignore it altogether and hope that the numbers game will work out in their favor. Years ago I was giving a proposal-writing workshop and met a young Marketing Coordinator from a firm in Texas. Using the "If it moves, we'll shoot at it" philosophy, her firm sent out 125 proposals a month! Of course with that strategy you inevitably discover that someone else has been there, making friends for a long time and you don't stand a chance.

Some firms use the "Rainmaker" approach—the hired gun who knows everyone, was a successful salesman in a previous career and is sent out to "bring back work." But clients want to get to know the people who are going to be responsible for getting the project done. They see the rainmaker as someone who'll toss the project over the fence and go out looking for more and "who knows whose hands I'll be left in?"

We also see the "Door-Opener" model, which uses an individual who is popular or connected in the right circles. This person is asked to introduce the technical staff to key contacts and kick-start these "arranged marriages." Since the door-opener never closes a deal, firms invariably begin to wonder about the return on their investment and the door-opener is gone.

Other firms use the "Seller-Doer" method. This is, in fact, the most common approach to business development. It puts the burden on the project managers and technical staff to feed themselves. While it addresses the inherent problem of the rainmaker, it results in a hunter-gatherer, "eat-what-you-kill" situation with constant conflict between nurturing your relationships and getting your work done.

## What's the best approach?

By themselves, none of these models work. Business development is a team sport and you need every one of these people playing for you. While there is usually a primary contact responsible for the relationship, the rainmaker needs the project delivery team, the project manager needs someone to scan the horizon for opportunities and we all need friends who can get us in the door.

So how does all this translate into your day-to-day activities? At the end of the day your client or prospect wants to know whether or not you care about him. Why? First, because people just enjoy being cared about. Second, because she wants to know whether, when things get rough, which they inevitably will, will you look out for her or for yourself?

Business development is about showing you care: if your trip takes you close by her office, stop in just to say "Hello." Clip an article from the newspaper that you think she might enjoy and send it along. Remember what college she went to and, when her team wins, send a congratulatory note. Ask about how her kids are doing in school or her Mom is doing following the operation. When the project meeting is done, ask if she has time for a cup of coffee and talk topics outside the project. Even if she can't let you pay for it, the time spent together *not* talking about the project is invaluable.

## Business development is like love

Remember back in high school when you were desperately in love with someone and that someone didn't even know you were on the face of the planet? What did you do?

Your high school quandary is a lot like the one you're facing now. There are people out there with whom you'd love to work, but they don't even know you exist. There are also prospects out there who know you're around but haven't recognized how talented and easy to work with you are.

Back in the high school love game, there were two schools of thought. The first group believed that love was a numbers game. If you simply asked enough girls (please excuse this seemingly sexist viewpoint, but after all, I did go through high school as a guy!) to go out with you, sooner or later someone would agree. There were two major flaws with this technique. First, it had a very high failure rate. Second, sometimes the result was a good news–bad news situation. The good news was, you've found a date. The bad news was, she wasn't someone you want to spend an entire evening with!

The second school of thought took a longer-term approach to love. You spent time studying the range of available dates and settled on a particular candidate ahead of time. Then you set out to build a relationship. The first step was to get her to see that you existed: walk by her locker every day; recruit friends to make introductions; if she enjoys music, join the band; if it's sports, try out for the team. The next was to get that first conversation. Get yourself invited to the same parties and arrange to be her lab partner. In step three, you worked into expanded conversations as you sat with her at lunch in the cafeteria and arranged to "accidentally" cross paths on the street and invited her for a coffee or soda. By this time, she's become comfortable with you, you've found some things in common and, when you ask if she'd like to go to a movie on Saturday, the likelihood of her saying "Yes" was much higher.

## Life's like high school

It's remarkable how much life (and business development) is like high school. When we went to college, life was about being an expert. "Pay attention, become an expert in this narrow field, and you'll be successful." But it turns out that life is like high school. There, success was measured by how you got along with people, how much and how many people liked and trusted you and wanted you in their group.

There are a lot of experts out there. Let's call them your competitors. But life and business development are like high school.

# 4

# Should You or Shouldn't You?

How would you like to double your hit rate? Overnight?

Simple. Just cut the number of RFPs your respond to and proposals you submit in half.

All joking aside, just about every firm I've ever dealt with writes too many proposals. In a world where relationships are key, far too many firms get suckered into submitting expensive proposals that they know they have no chance of winning. Your first step in writing a proposal that is wired to win is to stop writing ones that are likely to lose.

The trouble is the decision of whether to chase a project or not is a tough one. The one guarantee is, if you don't chase it, you won't win it. As a result, many firms shoot at anything that moves figuring that if they submit enough proposals they are bound to win some. That's the same school of thought that, in the dating game, says if I simply walk up to enough women and ask them to go out with me, sooner or later someone is bound to accept. It's simply a numbers game.

Unfortunately in both dating and proposal-writing, it's an expensive, time-consuming and frustrating process that often produces those good news/bad news results: the good news is you won a project. The bad news is that it's with *that* client, under those ridiculous contract terms, to design that questionable project.

Among the many advantages of cutting down the number of proposals you write is the fact that you will now have the time to invest in the proper research, writing, designing and producing a much higher quality proposal than you've ever done before. No more of those last minute panics as you wonder if the search-and-replace function in MS Word has actually found all instances of the name of the last client to whom you sent this same proposal last week.

Imagine how much better your proposal will look and read when it's the only one due this Friday instead of the three that you've often had to juggle before. Other benefits of cutting down the number of proposals you write include:

- You get to be selective about choosing the clients that will be a good fit for your firm.

- The stress levels for you and your marketing team will be much lower.

- Fewer mistakes will be made in the proposal documents and you'll have time for the quality control that can catch those few mistakes.

- Your proposals will be precisely targeted to each specific opportunity rather than a generic re-write of something sort of similar.

- By turning down poorly aligned opportunities, you position your firm more strongly in the marketplace.

- Your overhead costs for proposal-writing will be lower.

- You will have more time to spend building and reinforcing relationships that turn into sole-source or preferred provider work and reduce or eliminate competition.

Yes, it's always tempting to decide to go after that questionable job because, after all, what if there are no more jobs out there to chase? What if our backlog starts to shrink? How will I keep all these employees busy? While these fears are real, our imaginations tend to make them much more frightening than they actually are. In fact, increasing the quality and focus of the proposals you do choose to write is a much more effective way of dealing with these risks anyway.

So, in spite of the temptation, from now on you're going to be sufficiently wise and disciplined to go after only those projects that are a really good fit for your firm. You're going to cut down on the number of proposals you write at the same time that you dramatically increase the chances of winning the ones you do submit.

# A rational approach to doubling your hit rate

Once you've accepted the notion that a smaller number of proposals will lead to a larger number of wins, the next step is to remove the emotion from the "go/no-go" decision and make that process totally objective. Far too often I've seen bad decisions made purely on emotion, usually either fear or greed. Given that these are the two emotions that dominate in places like Las Vegas, let's decide to abandon them now as decision criteria.

The go/no-go process we're talking about is entirely rational. It is designed to remove that emotional influence and ensure that you are acting on solid evidence and good judgment. Using these techniques, it's actually quite easy to arrive at a sensible decision. What you do after that is up to you. You may decide that you're going to go after it anyway, and I have no problem with that. But at least you'll be doing it with your eyes wide open.

The go/no-go decision process has three parts:

1.  A "first glance" evaluation in which you make a broad-brush decision either to say "No" to the opportunity immediately or to take the time to investigate it further.
2.  A brief investigation into both the project and the client to evaluate the opportunity in more depth.
3.  A detailed evaluation process that will yield a numerical score and give you rational basis for your final decision.

# The first glance evaluation

This quick assessment asks a series of key questions about the project and the client and assigns a numerical score to your simple "Yes" or "No" answer. Five questions address "big" issues and another 10 address lesser ones.

**Big Issues.** Score 10 points for each "Yes" and 0 points for each "No." If your answer is "I don't know" either score 0 points or do some research to find out.

4.  Have we done a successful project with this client before?
5.  Is the project within our defined target markets?

6. Do we have a successful track record with this type of project?
7. Is it likely that we will make a profit on this project?
8. Does the client have the money to pay for us and the project?

**Lesser Issues.** Score 5 points for each "Yes" and 0 points for each "No." If your answer is "I don't know" either score 0 points or do some research to find out.

9. Do we have an established relationship with this client?
10. Is there a high likelihood of future opportunities from this project or this client?
11. Does this project have a high profile?
12. Is the selection process fair and reasonable?
13. Is selection based on qualifications and not low fee?
14. Do we have the project manager, the personnel, and the time to get the work done?
15. Is the schedule reasonable?
16. Are we well-positioned against the competition?
17. Is the project within our established geographic region?
18. Is the fee in excess of our minimum fee goals?

Add up your total score.

### 85–100

It seems the project has your name on it. This is your ideal project and you should put your best effort into pursuing it. But be careful not to be complacent! Phrases such as "It's ours to lose" tend to become self-fulfilling prophecies.

### 60–84

It's likely you have a good chance, but so do other firms. Research the project well, make sure you are covered by a good contract, and keep your eyes open for other opportunities.

### 40–59

This is not a high priority project for your sales efforts. Chase it if you want, but watch your costs carefully.

### Less than 40

You should thank the client for inviting you but politely decline the opportunity. It's more trouble than it's worth.

## Brief investigation

If your initial score is high enough to warrant going further, your next step is to invest some time evaluating both the client and the RFP for clues that could help in your ultimate evaluation and in preparing your response.

## Checking the RFP for clues

It's often the case that clients use the same techniques for writing their RFPs as you do for writing your proposals—they simply copy the most recent one and then change the appropriate names and facts. Nonetheless, there are usually clues that you can uncover by reading both the content and between the lines of the RFP that are not only useful in determining your go/no-go decision, but in crafting your proposal if you do choose to chase the project.

The examples that follow are all taken from actual RFPs issued by clients seeking to retain architecture, engineering, environmental or construction services.

The manner in which the RFP is written can give you insight into the project. For example:

If the RFP is written in very precise language it can be a clue that the client is ultimately going to select on price.

> *"The scope of work includes locking the three buildings together structurally, providing shear collectors in the floors, adding shear walls, securing parapets, securing brick veneer to structure, securing mechanical/electrical equipment, and modifying foundations under shear walls. Alternate solutions will be considered if they provide a cost savings and do not adversely affect the project schedule."*

A client who doesn't have much project experience may write an RFP that reflects their inexperience and ignorance of the process. This could result in either trouble as you spend time educating them, or opportunity as they pay for additional services.

> *"These qualifications should indicate all projects worked on during the last ten (10) years and include the name of the project, dates and specific items worked on."*

An RFP that reflects a client who is has a great deal of project experience could foreshadow trouble down the road and indicate the need for tough negotiations and a good contract.

> *"All work products of the A/E that result from this contract are the exclusive property of ABC Bank, including the right of copyright of any published work."*

An RFP that is poorly written and unclear could represent a client who is in need of consulting services beyond those in the RFP. It might also indicate someone who is looking for free ideas.

> *"The selected firm will provide all necessary resources to complete or perform the specific duties involved in working with the Leisure Center Committee in the development of a public process to best determine the community needs for aquatic and recreation facilities."*

You can often sniff out a project that is already wired to someone else when the RFP specifies selection criteria that don't seem connected to the job. There may also be a very short time frame in which to respond.

> *"The selected Engineering consultant shall:*
>
> * *Provide and maintain a local project office within 10 blocks of the project site.*
> * *Provide a project manager who has a minimum 15 years experience on projects of this sort.*
> * *Demonstrate an in-depth knowledge of the strategic planning issues that have led to the implementation of this project."*

Wired projects can also appear to have been written by someone who obviously has professional level knowledge about the project and its issues beyond what a normal client might have.

> *"Provide new chillers or Owner-approved alternates. Repair and modify fans as required. Continue to use the existing commingled steam supply from the adjacent building. Replace the duct system in the two buildings and provide replacement in the main branch building in conjunction with the partial abatement of asbestos."*

# Checking the client for clues

While the RFP document will give you clues about whether or not this project is right for you, speaking with the client will also provide considerable insight. More often than not today, especially with larger, more sophisticated clients, there is a ban on speaking with anyone except the designated spokesperson within the client's organization once the RFP hits the street. Nonetheless, you can usually judge the level of the client's willingness to take a "team" approach by the way they respond to your inquiries—and you definitely will want to make inquiries. Too many firms base their entire response on information in the RFP (and perhaps additional information they learned at the all-consultants' meeting). Make it a habit to dig as deep as you can and unearth as much information and insight as possible.

It's in your best interest to look for clients who are:

- Willing to sit down and openly discuss the project with you.

   *"The City wishes to retain a firm that can demonstrate its ability to provide an effective team that will supply the City with architectural and community consultative services. The location and specific design of the leisure center have not yet been determined. The Consultant will work with the Leisure Center Committee to facilitate those decisions."*

- Willing to share information about the project.

   *"Please contact John Doe if more information is needed or to provide comments on this project."*

   *"Arrangements may be made for pre-interview inspections of the site through the primary contact person."*

- Flexible about how they work with you.

   *"For those invited to interview, the interview format and presentation is at the discretion of the consultant."*

- Willing to let you in on information which will be helpful in your submission.

   *"To assist in the preparation of the Statement of Qualifications, a draft of the Request for Proposal which defines the Scope of Work is available at the City Hall, Department of Environmental Services."*

And always be wary of clients who are not interested in learning about you and your firm.

> *"The consultant is advised that contact with University officials regarding this project without clearance with the primary contact may lead to disqualification from the consultant selection process."*

In general, always keep your eyes and ears open for clues that suggest that the client or the project may be easier or more difficult that it appears on the surface. Let your observations and your gut instincts influence your go/no-go decision.

# The decision

It's commitment time.

Being fully honest and using all the insight you've gathered in your investigations, go through the following comprehensive checklist to evaluate the project. Watch especially for those items marked with an asterisk, which indicates a potential deal buster. If you answer "No" to any of these questions, think long and hard before spending big money to pursue the project.

### About the client

1.  Have we dealt with this client before?
2.  *Is the client financially stable? Does the client have a good business reputation?
3.  *Does this client pay their bills promptly?
4.  Is this the type of project the client has worked on before both successfully and regularly?
5.  *Is the client willing to spend the necessary time with us to fully discuss the project prior to preparing the proposal?
6.  Are there future opportunities with this client?
7.  Do we know who makes the final decision?
8.  Would our other clients approve of our involvement with this project?
9.  *Is the client realistic about the schedule and budget?

**About the project**

10. *Do we have (or can we get) a well-defined scope of work?

11. Can the permits and approvals be obtained within the client's planned time frame?

12. Are we familiar with all the applicable regulations and technologies?

13. Are there future opportunities for similar projects with other clients?

14. Have we worked on projects like this before, both successfully and regularly?

15. *Do we have a project manager with experience in this type of project?

16. Are we sure our work load will not be strained by taking on this project at this time?

17. *Do we have at least as much chance to be selected as our competitors?

18. Can we comply with the time schedule for completing our portion of the work?

19. *Can we provide high-quality client service on this project?

**Your business considerations**

20. *Is this what our business and marketing plans say we should be doing?

21. Is the selection process reasonable?

22. *Do we have a strong message that will differentiate us from the competition?

23. Will the project be worth the marketing effort it takes to get it?

24. Can we comply with any MBE, WBE, DBE requirements?

25. Will the client agree to a contract with a limitation of liability clause?

26. *Will the contract with the client be equitable?

27. Will the contract be free of hold-harmless and indemnity provisions?

28. Will the contract be free of speculative aspects?

29. *Will our fee be wholly adequate? Profitable?

30. Is there a good reason to take this job if we don't anticipate a profit?

31. Will our fee be competitive?

32. Is the owner willing to provide funds for unexpected contingencies?

33. Have we checked the insurance requirements and found no special insurance needs?

34. *Should we be investing our resources in this a project?

35. *Is this the best opportunity we have at this time?

Count up your "Yes" answers.

**30 or more**

Go for it with all you've got.

**25–30**

Make sure your proposal has strong differentiators.

**20–24**

Think twice about this. Your chances aren't very good.

**Less than 20**

Turn down the project.

# Closed Jobs Analysis (or Hindsight is 20/20)

Sometimes the go/no-go analysis can still advise you to chase a project that isn't right for you. Trying to guess how a particular project is going to work out is tough, but hindsight is always perfect. We can use statistics to help us identify projects that are more likely than not to be successful.

The process is called Closed Jobs Analysis and it provides insight that can be startling. As the name implies, the process involves analyzing projects that have been completed. The key is to look at all projects going back three to five years to observe trends in project performance. Here's how it works:

Using an Excel spreadsheet, collect all the pertinent data from *all* past projects going back from two to five years. Anything more recent than two years won't give you the information you need. Project data to collect includes:

- Client
- Client type
- Project type
- Project size
- Project manager
- Fee budget
- Profit

These are the basics, but you can enter more key data if you like. You then work with the spreadsheet to sort by the various criteria and look for patterns. For example, what happens to profit when sorted by Project Size? What happens to profit when sorted by Project Manager?

What can this show you? Here are stories from two firms to give you an indication of what you might discover.

Firm One conducted an analysis of all projects completed during the past three years. There were no patterns of profitability based on project type or client type, but when sorted by project size, the firm made a huge discovery. When looking at individual projects, those with total fees below $12,000 accounted for more than 35 percent of labor hours, but just 17 percent of profit. When the cutoff was raised to fees of $25,000, these accounted for almost 55 percent of labor hours, but just 22 percent of profits.

Stated another way, the firm could have worked about half the hours and still made more than 75 percent of the profit.

Firm Two also conducted an analysis of projects from the past three years. In their case project size had no impact on profitability, but project type was a huge influence. With fees totaling about $2.25 million after about 18,000 labor hours, profits were around 12 percent, at just under $270,000. But of six categories of project type, two of them, accounting for almost $350,000 in revenue and 5,000 hours of labor, did not make money on a single project. In fact they combined for a net loss of about $55,000.

The analysis showed that the vast majority of the firm's profits came from three of the six project types. If the three poor performers were eliminated completely the company's revenue would have dropped from $2.25 million to $1.3 million, labor hours would have dropped from 18,000 to less than 8,000 and profit would have *increased* from $270,000 to more than $320,000!

# What happens when you chase something you shouldn't?

We do it all the time. In spite of great research, common sense and our best instincts, we decide to go after the project anyway. If that's your decision, fine. But know what you're getting yourself into.

### The $1 million fee

A few years back, a call came from a firm that wanted help to win a particular project. They wanted to win this project more than anything else because it came with a fee of $1 million. This firm had never won a project with such a fee and the principals were drooling all over themselves. They had already planned where to spend every one of those million dollars. Then the time came to sit down and discuss the project and brainstorm for their win tactics.

They had first heard of the job more than a year before when they'd been awarded a small feasibility study that preceded it. While the study didn't pay big bucks, they understood that it could lead to the larger project. Their strategy was to use the feasibility study as a marketing opportunity to win the big prize. The tactic was to pull out all the stops and make the study better than anyone would ever expect. The results were fabulous and the client was thrilled with their work.

However, as always, there was a catch.

The fee they were paid for the feasibility study was $15,000 while the firm's cost to put together this study-of-all-studies was $60,000. I pointed out that so far the firm was now $45,000 in the hole. Of course they were aware of this but felt no cause for concern because, "after all, what's $45,000 compared to a $1 million fee?"

I then asked about the status of the project. Was it real? Did the client have the money to build it? Everything seemed to be in place with one small exception. The bond issue had yet to be passed. Now the passing of a bond issue is a very big deal. When we got down to a realistic probability of the bond passing, the firm guessed 50-50. Their enthusiasm went down a notch.

Moving on we then talked about another potential deal buster: the competition. "Is this project," I asked, "wired for you? Is it yours, assuming the bond referendum passes?"

They 'fessed up that there was one other firm in the running but that since they had performed the feasibility study, their chances of beating the other firm were still very good. We chatted some more, and they put the odds at 70–30.

We need now to briefly go back to introductory statistics and combine the two probabilities (50 percent chance of passing the bond and 70 percent chance of beating the competition). This puts the overall likelihood of landing the project at just 35 percent. Having not looked at things this way before, their smiles faded.

We then switched the topic to profitability. The firm was not terribly efficient and typically saw a profit of 8 or 9 percent on their projects. This project would be a little out of the ordinary for them and demanded a learning curve. We agreed to estimate a 5 percent profit margin on the job.

Some quick arithmetic tells us that five percent of $1 million is $50,000. Since the firm was already $45,000 in the hole, assuming that no other mistakes of any sort were made, the best they could hope to profit from the job was $5,000.

Let's go to the horse track to sum this situation up.

- They put a $45,000 bet on a horse.
- The horse had less than 4-in-10 odds of winning.
- There was no payout for 2nd or 3rd place (unlike an actual horse race).
- And, if their horse did actually win, it would pay out a mere $5,000.

Would you put a bet on a horse like this?

Even without going into a detailed go/no-go evaluation it is easy to see through the tempting $1 million fee to the unnecessary risk and hassle the proposal really represented.

The end of the story?

Sometimes fairytales do come true. The bond passed and the firm won the job and was successful with the project.

## The $5,000 loser

This story is about a particular firm. It could, however, be about your firm or any other firm out there.

This firm—we won't use any names here—had heard about a new project that seriously interested them. They did a little research and discovered that this client fit right into their target market profile and would make an ideal long-term customer.

Since they had not worked for this client before and had established no relationship, they knew they had little hope of winning. They did, however, want to begin the relationship process with the client in hopes of winning later projects.

Using a reasoning process that is all too common, they decided to submit a proposal on the project. They figured that, while their chances of winning the project were slim to none, it would help position them with the prospective client and help build the relationship.

But there is a serious flaw in that very common reasoning.

The average cost to produce a proposal on a project is about $5,000. This average includes those low-cost "confirmation letter" proposals that you send to current clients as well as the full-blown efforts that can cost tens of thousands of dollars. So this firm spent about $5,000 to position themselves with this client.

But what position did they establish?

As the last story pointed out, the business development process is not like a horse race. In a horse race you at least get money for your bet if your horse comes first, second, or third. In this race, you either come first, or you might as well come dead last.

The point is, in this business, you either win . . . or you lose. Coming in "second" is just the first of the losers.

So what had this firm accomplished with their $5,000? They succeeded in positioning themselves with this prospect as one of the losers. Why is this common tactic such a bad idea? Because it uses the wrong tool for the job.

A proposal is a tool designed specifically for sales. It does not do well as a tool for brand building and positioning, which is a completely different undertaking. There are other tools that are better suited for positioning your firm with one or many prospects. If this firm had $5,000 to spend, they should have spent it more effectively on some public relations, some advertising or perhaps some direct mail. Then, after they had successfully positioned themselves in the mind of the prospect, they could spend the money to chase a project and have a much higher likelihood of winning.

# 5

# Playing Detective

Once you have decided that the project is worth the time and money to pursue, the next step is to collect as much information about the client, the project, the selection process, the competition, and the surrounding circumstances as possible. Every bit of information you can get your hands on is valuable. It may not seem so at the time, but information is the key to success in sales and the more you have, the better position you will be in.

In this process of investigation you want to be looking as much for the intangible things as you are for the "hard" information. Yes, you want to find out about schedules, budgets, scopes of work and technical specifications. But you also want to learn about personalities, political winds that might be blowing, hidden agendas and alliances and all other behind-the-scenes insight that you can gather.

The more you know about your customer and their project, the better are your chances of winning. This means you must know them in depth despite the hurdles you may encounter. This section gives you a target list of information you should try to collect and some techniques for getting that information.

## Set a deadline!

A vital key to the research step is to give yourself a time limit. There will always be more information that you can dig up, but at some point you have to take the material you have collected and move forward with your capture plan.

Depending on the project, your time limit might be two weeks, two days or two hours. It doesn't matter. Set the limit, dig as fast and as deep as you can, then stop and work with the material you have collected.

# Things to discover . . .

## About the client

> What is their business?
>
> How does it operate?
>
> Who are the key decision makers?
>
> What are their overt or covert agendas?
>
> Do different decision makers have different overt or covert agendas?
>
> How large is the company (or agency)?
>
> Are they growing, holding steady, or shrinking?
>
> Who are the key people in the organization?
>
> What are their roles?
>
> Is there a strong "personality" to the organization?
>
> What is the history of the company?
>
> What are the company's main strengths?
>
> What are their current weaknesses?
>
> Do you have any contacts in this organization?
>
> Do you know anyone who has a strong connection with them?
>
> Can you arrange an introduction with them?
>
> Have they worked with other design firms before?
>
> What is their level of sophistication on projects?
>
> What are their expectations?
>
> Do they emphasize service and quality or price?
>
> Do we (or could we) use any of their products or services?
>
> Do they compete with any of our other clients?

## About the project

> What is the history of this project's development?
>
> What is the project supposed to accomplish for the owners?
>
> What is it supposed to accomplish for the users?

Does the project represent a significant step in the growth of the client's organization?

Does the project have any particular "patrons" in the client's organization?

Does it have any enemies in the organization?

Does the project break new ground for the client or their industry?

Has a site been selected already?

If so, can you visit it?

Can you visit a similar, existing facility and speak with the users?

How will the project be funded?

Is the funding already secured?

Are there any significant political issues or special interest groups involved with the project?

What are the design and technical challenges on the project?

Are their any precedents for meeting challenges of this sort?

What specialty disciplines will be needed?

Does the client already have certain people or firms in mind to supply these special needs?

## About the selection process

How will the selection be made?

What are the stated selection criteria?

Who has determined these selection criteria?

Do you have any reason to believe the actual selection criteria may differ from what are stated?

If so, what are the real selection criteria?

What is the relative weighting of each selection point?

Are they looking for "new and exciting" or "standard and safe?"

Who is on the selection committee?

What do you know about each person on the committee?

What have they liked in the past?

Is there any political wrangling on the committee?

Who is in charge of the committee?

Whose opinion carries the most weight on the committee?

What is their opinion?

What are the expectations regarding size, sophistication and content of the proposal and interview?

Are there specific minority participation requirements for the project?

What are the required (stated) percentages as opposed to the desired (unstated) percentages?

Which are the most talented minority firms to consider working with?

Which are the most "politically correct" minority firms to consider working with?

Does this client "spread the work around" evenly?

If so, is it your turn?

## About the competition

What firms do you expect to compete against for this project?

Who do you expect to be the primary competition?

What services do they offer?

What are their strengths?

What are their weaknesses?

What kind of reputation do they have in the market?

Who are the partners in these firms?

What do we know about each one?

Who are their key staff members?

Which consultants do they typically work with?

What level of quality do they produce?

Are they technically adequate, competent, or superior?

Is their design work adequate, competent, or superior?

What is their present workload?

Have they won any significant awards?

Which projects are they known for?

Have they made any major blunders in the past that may still haunt them?

What is their attitude towards this project?

# Where to find all this information

That's a big list and it's highly unlikely you will be able to check off every item. However, if you are scratching your head, wondering where on earth you could find out some of this information, ask yourself if you have:

Asked the client directly

Spoken with their peers

Checked with former employees

Searched on the Internet

Talked to mutual contractors or consultants

Looked in the Who's Who directory

Checked your LinkedIn or other Internet contacts

Looked carefully at the stuff hanging on the walls of their office

Checked the local library

Searched on the Internet

Asked a mutual client

Checked the industry association meetings or journals

Gone to the Chamber of Commerce

Collected and read their brochures and marketing materials

Received a shareholder prospectus about the company

Searched on the Internet

Looked in the appropriate trade journals

Reviewed appropriate industrial directories

Read their Annual Report

Spoken with staff at the regulatory and permitting agencies

Talked with other vendors and suppliers who deal with them

Checked their ad in the Yellow Pages

Run a Dun & Bradstreet report

Did I mention searching on the Internet?

## Some additional techniques

Gathering all this information can be a daunting task. But there's an entire profession dedicated to collecting and reporting hard-to-find information in very short periods of time–Investigative Journalists. The techniques they use are wonderfully effective and can serve you just as well as you attempt to get the inside story on that elusive client.

Here are some tactics you can try in your efforts to be the next Woodward and Bernstein.

### Six degrees of separation

Like Will Smith in the movie of that title, investigative journalists have always believed that it takes just six steps to connect you with any other human being on the face of the earth. It works like this:

I want to be introduced to the Director of Facilities of the Acme Corporation. First, I will need a compelling reason so the people I ask will be motivated to assist me.

Next, I ask someone that I know whether they know someone who knows the Director of Facilities of the Acme Corporation and could introduce me. Predictably, they don't. But then I ask if they know anyone who knows anything about the Acme Corporation who might be able to put me a step closer. They remember that their neighbor down the street has a job in a similar industry. He might be of assistance.

I call the neighbor, explain how I was given his name, and ask if he knows anyone who might be able to help. He's glad to give me the name of a sales rep who regularly calls on Acme and with whom he had been dealing. I call or email that person and ask them the same question. And on it goes until I succeed in getting the introduction.

A good journalist can connect themselves to the right information source with a very few phone calls. They whittle down the number of connections by maintaining a thick file of friendly sources they have built up over the years. Today we call it "networking." Your network is also extensive. (Hint: That's why you signed up with LinkedIn.) You just have to start using it to collect and direct you to information.

## The scavenger hunt

This technique is useful when you have to delegate the information-gathering duties. It can be very effective in short periods of time. The object of the game is to see who can collect the most information in a fixed period of time.

Assign two junior staff members to the task. You can even make use of your receptionist's time in this exercise. Give them both a quick outline of the project and a copy of the lists from above, and explain that their task is to collect as much information about the client, the project, the competition, or anything regarding the project as they can before the time is up. Then give them a deadline. Don't make it too far in the future, a few hours or a day works fine. If they have too long a period, they will get distracted and lose focus.

Using the techniques from the Six Degrees of Separation and whatever resources they can muster, they must collect and record information. Each person has access to a phone, a computer, the library, and whatever information sources are available to the firm. Tell them that they are an ace reporter and they have a hot story due on the 6:00 news. Then let them go at it.

The winner—the one who comes back with the most information of any sort related to the items on your list—gets dinner for two at the nicest restaurant in town.

## The all consultants' meeting

Most clients hold an "all consultants' meeting" in which they discuss the project and answer any questions you might have. The typical approach to these meetings is that everyone sits quietly, listens to the client talk about the project, and asks very few, if any, questions.

Everyone's afraid to say anything in case they give away their closely guarded secrets and their competitive edge. But the net result is that every consultant leaves the meeting knowing exactly the same information as everyone else. Valuable questions are left unasked and unanswered and the client is left wondering if any of the consultants even have a pulse or if anyone was awake.

At your next all consultants' meeting, take a different approach. Instead of sitting quietly, go in with a long list of questions. Dominate the meeting with your questions and don't worry about giving away any "inside information." Ask all the questions you want. Make them insightful and challenging. Of course, don't challenge the client's integrity or intelligence, just show that you want to know everything there is to know about this project.

At the end of the meeting everyone will still walk out, all knowing the same information. (If they've been paying attention. Some won't.) But what will the client know about you? They'll know that you represent an aggressive firm who is determined to be thorough, persistent and accurate. They'll know you're different from everyone else because you took a deep and genuine interest in their project. They'll be looking forward to receiving your proposal.

## Going down the ladder

When a client issues an RFP, it usually names a contact person who will dispense the information they feel consultants require. The difficulty is this contact person will only ever give you the "official" answers and will make sure that everyone else is given the answers to the insightful questions you ask.

You have to find a "back door" into the organization that will allow you to gain important insights into the company and perhaps even the project that aren't influenced by the "company line." The most effective way to do this is to go further down in the organization and speak with someone at the operations level—someone, preferably without a title, who isn't shy about telling you what's really going on. Take the janitor to lunch. No one has ever done that before and they will be so thrilled they will be happy to tell you anything you want to know. And you'd be surprised at the number of conversations they overhear.

For example, I was once helping a firm with a proposal for a multi-modal transit center in a city in North Carolina. The client was holding their cards very close to their chest and being quite uncooperative when it came to revealing insights into what was really behind the project. I took an afternoon and visited the existing transit center where all the local buses connected. I found a supervisor whose job it was to coordinate the comings and goings of all the buses. We had a very nice 45-minute conversation and I gained a great deal of insight about the project from the operations level that we were able to successfully incorporate into our proposal.

This back door approach will almost always provide you with insights that you will never get dealing with the "gatekeepers." An effective way of building lower-level connection is to have your technical staff communicate with the client's technical staff. They have a professional camaraderie which can cross corporate lines and provide you with a vital link to critical information.

But be careful not to abuse this connection. It would be risky to both your firm and the person with whom you speak.

## Ignoring the rules

Despite the fact that most RFPs tell you not to speak with the members of the selection committee, it's worth considering anyway. At the very least, call or write simply to introduce yourself, let them know that you will be submitting a proposal and are looking forward to speaking and dealing with them.

You never know, you just might gain an insight into their thoughts or feelings about the project. If someone does agree to speak with you, don't spend your time selling your firm to them. Instead, concentrate on their feelings. Listen carefully to what they want to talk about. Start off by asking some probing questions and then spend most of the time listening to the answers. Don't push your firm. Instead, find out what they are thinking and worried about.

By contacting the selection committee members you may run the risk of being disqualified from the project. If that is a possibility, don't risk it. Only try this if you determine that you can make a positive impression during the conversation.

## Keep a dossier on your competitors

Whenever Apple comes out with a new computer, the first ones off the line are purchased by Microsoft, Dell, Gateway and the other computer manufacturers. Why? Certainly not because they want a new computer. They buy them and instantly start dismantling them, reverse-engineering the systems and features of the computer and doing an in-depth analysis of the pricing strategy and packaging. They do this because they cannot survive without detailed information about the activities and strategies of their top competitors.

Neither can you.

If you want to be an effective player in the market, you must know what is going on with your competition. While you should not move into "reactive" mode and make all your decisions based on what they are doing, neither can you ignore your competitors.

Every design firm should maintain a file (let's call it a dossier, it sounds so much more like James Bond!) on each of their main competitors. In it you should have a print-out of their current web site, a copy of their brochure and a list of the partners and key employees along with their outline résumés. You should also add any other pertinent information that you can discover, such as key clients, project histories, known strengths and weaknesses, recent hires and employees who have left the company.

While it sounds like an impossible task to gather this information, it is not as difficult as it seems. The design profession is a relatively small world. It's highly likely that someone who is working in your firm has spent time working for your competitor. Interview them. Find out why they left. Ask what is good and bad about their former employer. Your clients, contractors and sub-consultants also have information about them. They probably have a brochure lying around somewhere, too. Start asking and digging and you'll be amazed at what you can find!

Don't be afraid that word will get back to the competitor that you have been asking about them—it will. But so what? Apple knows that Toshiba and Dell are buying their computers. It's just part of doing business.

The reason you want this information is to help you get wired more closely to your clients. If you know that you are likely to go up against a certain competitor when pursuing a project, you can fine-tune your effort either to take advantage of a weakness of the competitor or to guard against a strength. How does this work?

Let's say you have decided to chase a new water treatment plant project for a local municipality. Your research has told you that one of your main competitors has recently given a seminar at the regional American Public Works Association conference that was very well received. This could give them a strong advantage since the local public works director would be impressed with their obvious expertise. With this knowledge you might:

1. Mount an extra effort to build on your own relationship with the public works director.

2. Conduct a short, direct-mail program in which you send a series of tips on state-of-the-art treatment plant maintenance and technology to the ten Public Works Directors within a 50-mile radius.

3. Investigate the idea of pursuing the project as a joint venture with the competitor.

4. Look outside your area to connect with a nationally-known consultant who presented an even more impressive seminar.

There may be another strategy you choose, but the point is each of these strategies acknowledges the reality of the marketplace. Without this information you would walk in blind and then wonder why the other firm won.

# War Stories

## The project that wasn't there

I was asked to give a proposal-writing workshop to a firm on the West Coast. I suggested that they would get the most from the workshop if we could work with an actual RFP to which they were going to respond. We could spend the day actually writing the proposal.

When I arrived at eight o'clock that morning, the RFP was sitting on the table. I assumed they had some background so we began the discussion by me asking questions about the project.

"Who is this client?"

"It's a municipality about 20 miles away."

"Have we worked for them before?"

"No."

"Then how did we get the RFP?"

"It came in the mail."

"But how did this client decide to send it to us?"

"We don't know."

"How did this client get our name?"

"We don't know."

"Who else has been asked to respond?"

"We don't know."

By this time it was obvious the firm knew little or nothing about the client, the project, the selection process or the competition. But, as often happens, they were about to spend almost $5,000 to prepare and submit a proposal that would be nothing more than a shot in the dark. I could not go along with it.

I called for a break and went off with the marketing coordinator and a secretary to play Scavenger Hunt. (See the description of this game above.) They were each given a phone and 20 minutes. Their assignment: find out anything and everything about this project. They began dialing.

Twenty minutes later they had found out that:

- The client, a municipality about 20 miles away, was merely "thinking about" doing the project.

- The project was only a dream and no funding was in place.

- The RFP was simply intended to "kick some tires" and get feedback on costs to determine if they would actually be able to do the project.

- The firm was one of twelve that had been invited to submit proposals.

- The client had been given the firm's name by a sub-consultant who had also submitted the names of four other prime consultants.

In short, they found out enough in 20 minutes to decide without hesitation that the project did not warrant the effort and expense of a proposal. We reconvened and drafted a short letter of regret to the client.

The punch line to this story is that the firm's principals then told me they were glad we decided not to pursue the project because now we had time to work on another, *really* important proposal they had to prepare!

# The "wired" construction project

I was asked to help a construction company pursue a project. It was a major renovation and reconstruction of laboratories and office buildings for a telecommunications company. The project was worth $100 million and, needless to say, was a very big deal for the company.

We did a little research on the project and the client, but, unfortunately, did not have (or take!) the time to research the competition. Everything looked reasonable, but a little voice in my head kept telling me that something was odd. The client seemed to have a very close relationship with one competitor and my instinct told me the project was already wired to them. With no hard evidence however, there was no way I could talk myself or the construction company out of pursuing the project.

My client was made for this job. They were head-and-shoulders more qualified and experienced than anybody else. We put together a very impressive proposal and made the short list. We put on a blow-your-socks-off interview that went extremely well by anyone's standards. And then we waited.

Finally, after three weeks of inexplicable silence on the part of the client, they announced that, "subject to the firm putting together a team capable of running the project," the job was awarded to the competitor! No, I'd never heard that one before either.

The politics of their relationship was so strong that, despite the fact that the competitor could not show that they could do such a big project, they were awarded it anyway!

There are two key lessons to take away from this story. First, trust your instincts. If something smells fishy, it probably is. Pay attention to your gut feeling and take the time to dig a little deeper. Second, no matter how good you are, you'll never have a 100 percent hit rate. So pick yourself up, dust yourself off, and get on with your other opportunities.

# 6

# Capture Strategy

Now that you have gathered as much information as possible about the project, the client and the competition, you are almost ready to prepare and launch the capture strategy in earnest.

A capture strategy or plan consists of the specific actions you intend to use to win the project. This includes the content of your proposal, the information and points you intend to emphasize and the manner in which you package and present your information. The premise of the vast majority of capture plans is:

> *"If I give you enough information about myself, my firm and what we have done for others, you will be able to extrapolate and make assumptions about what we can do for you."*

Unfortunately, potential clients (in their role as egocentric human beings) get tired of reading and hearing about you and want to hear more about themselves. They will usually give up reading about you because they lose interest. Besides, reading about you is just like reading about every other consultant in the pile of proposals. Every proposal has long lists of projects. Each proposal has very similar-looking résumés. Every proposal states that the firm is uniquely qualified.

Wouldn't you get tired of reading this stuff? (More about that in the next chapter!)

How then, can you craft a message that not only holds the client's interest but actually convinces them that they should hire you? It's not as difficult as you might think.

This next step is likely not one you've commonly taken. And while it might be unusual, it's not terribly difficult and it is by far the most critical step to crafting an effective capture plan.

## The brainstorming session

For this critical exercise you must gather the key members of the project team into a room for a short brainstorming session. It should take no more than one hour, but I can't overemphasize the importance of this meeting.

Who should be present?

- The principal who is responsible for the client.
- The marketing person who has been following the effort.
- The project manager who will likely take the project through to completion.
- Any key staff members who will be involved with the project.
- Anyone else who may have additional information and insight into the client and the project.

In some cases, this long list will add up to just one person. In others, it might be four or five people. Regardless, gather this group and get them thinking.

## A brainstorm about brainstorming

Do you know what one of the best brainstorming mediums is? Plate glass windows.

If your office or boardroom has big, expansive windows, you're in luck. Because windows act just like dry-erase white boards. But they're a whole lot bigger! And, they offer the added bonus of feeling like you're being slightly naughty when you write on them. This frees up your creative spirits and let's you arrive at all manner of off-the-wall ideas.

I have brainstormed on so many windows over my career. We have filled entire window walls with notes. And the best part is that I'm usually working with the project team and we're making great progress when the CEO walks in to see how we're doing. He or she will usually pause, scratch their head, and then walk back out without saying a word.

You might have white board space and go ahead and use it if you do, but it's usually limited so you're reluctant to use it for anything but the best ideas. But you don't know what the best ideas are going to be until you've

The purpose of this exercise is first to step outside of the normal process of writing standard sections in a proposal and then to step into the key issues that the client will consider when choosing the consultant for their project.

*Your answers to these questions will serve as the themes that run throughout your business development effort and ensure that your proposal is written in direct response to the client's agenda and their needs. In short, it will wire you to the client and the project.*

There are four very important questions to be answered by your brainstorming group. Refer to the information you discovered during your research so that your answers are accurate and not simply a "gut feel."

Each question is detailed on its own form in the following pages. Reproduce these forms or use a flip chart to record your answers. When you're done with each question, hang the sheets on the wall for the duration of your meeting.

collected dozens of ideas from which to select.

Dry erase markers wipe off glass even better than they do off white boards. Just remember not to use permanent markers!

**Question #1: What are the client's "hot buttons" on this project?**

Hot buttons are those key, pivotal issues that the decision makers will consider the most important in the execution of this project. Hot buttons come in many "flavors." On one project the overriding issue might be budget. The client must complete the project for as little cost as possible. On another it might be schedule, since a looming deadline makes on-time completion of the project imperative. A third project may be driven by political issues where an incumbent candidate depends on the project's successful completion as a major plank in an election campaign. And on yet another project, the key issues may be technical or design-related.

While there is often a single issue that dominates the others, there is rarely only one hot button. Your job is to identify all the hot buttons that are driving this particular project. List as many as you can think of and then, if there are a lot of them, prioritize them into from most important to least.

When you are finished, list the top five (or as many as you've found) on *Form #1* and hang it on the wall.

### *Example*

The project was to replace a bridge that crossed a toll highway. The existing bridge was old and beyond repair. The problem was that the toll highway had been built between the residential and the business sections of town, effectively isolating them from each other. With the bridge out of commission during construction, the only way to the business district was a three-mile detour. It was faster and more convenient to simply go to the business district of the next town. Business owners were furious about the project.

#### Key hot buttons on this project

1.  Schedule: Get the old bridge down and the new bridge up and open in as little time as possible.
2.  Community relations: Keep the businesses as informed as possible through this unfortunate process. If they feel they are in the dark, they will react very negatively. At the same time, try to keep the detour route as convenient as possible to keep traffic going to the main business district.
3.  Keeping traffic flowing on the toll highway: Although construction is going on above, closing the toll road is not an option.

**BRAINSTORMING QUESTION #1**

What are the primary 'hot buttons' that are the drivers behind this project?

Hot buttons are those key, pivotal issues that the key decision makers will consider the most important in the execution of this project. Hot buttons come in many 'flavors.' On one project the overriding issue might be budget. The client must complete the project for as little cost as possible. On another it might be schedule since a looming deadline makes on-time completion of the project imperative. A third project may be driven by political issues where an incumbent candidate depends on its successful completion as a major plank in an election campaign. And on yet another project the key issues may be technical or design related.

1. _____

2. _____

3. _____

4. _____

5. _____

6. _____

7. _____

8. _____

9. _____

10. _____

Have you considered:

| | |
|---|---|
| Technical issues | The approvals process |
| Construction costs | Site issues |
| Environmental concerns | The design |
| Politics | Scheduling |
| Professional fees | Quality control |
| Project management | Qualifications/experience |
| Project delivery methods | The project team |
| Interpersonal chemistry | |

When you have completed this form, hang it on the wall for reference during the preparation of the proposal and presentation.

While there were some additional, secondary hot buttons on this project, these three were by far the most important for success. You'll notice that budget was *not* included in the key list. Nor were there any technical issues regarding design or construction of the bridge. In this

**BRAINSTORMING QUESTION #2**

What are the capabilities, traits and tactics of the Ideal Firm for this client and this project?

You are the key decision maker in the client's organization. You are responsible for choosing the consultant to be used on this project. It's about 5:00 AM and you're lying in bed, half asleep, half awake. In your semi-dream state you are thinking about the project and the consultant you will hire to make it happen. You're not thinking about any particular consultant. Instead, your imagination has invented the perfect consultant, the one you would hire in a heartbeat. This consultant does not exist, except in your dream. But they represent everything you would ever want in a consultant. What is that firm like?

1. _____

2. _____

3. _____

4. _____

5. _____

6. _____

7. _____

8. _____

9. _____

10. _____

Have you considered:

| | |
|---|---|
| Technical capability | Personality traits |
| Cost control | Attitudes |
| Reputation | Design talent |
| Political connections | Pricing |
| Past relationships | Experience profile |
| Political correctness | |

When you have completed this form, hang it on the wall for reference during the preparation of the proposal and presentation.

case the bridge was quite straightforward and simple. Virtually any competent bridge engineer could easily design it.

So a firm that pursues this project by touting its strong technical capability and listing all the bridges they had designed would miss the point completely.

## Question #2: What are the traits of the "perfect firm" for this project?

Here's the situation: You are the key decision maker in the client's organization. You are responsible for choosing the consultant to be used on this project.

It's 5:00 AM and you're lying in bed, half asleep, half awake. In your semi-dream state you are thinking about the project and the consultant you will hire to make it happen. You're not thinking about any particular consultant. Instead, your imagination has invented the perfect consultant, the one you would hire in a heartbeat. This consultant does not exist, except in your dream. But the dream firm represents everything you would ever want in a consultant. What is that firm like?

List the traits of that firm on *Form #2* and hang it on the wall.

### *Example*

Let's look at the key decision-makers for two completely different clients.

Decision-maker A is a 48-year old state Department of Transportation employee. He has been a state employee all his career and has successfully risen to an upper management position. His pension is fully vested and he would like to move up two more steps in the ladder before taking early retirement at 57 or 58. This project is "his baby" and he's been nursing it through the system for two years. When it is finished, if everything goes well, he will likely be given his next promotion. What would the firm of his dreams look like?

1. They would, without being asked, work hard to make him look good to his superiors.
2. They would thoroughly understand and work within the department's bureaucratic process. There's nothing worse than having to teach a newcomer how "the system" works or having some hotshot who thinks they can bypass the process.
3. They would be a known entity that has been tried and tested on previous projects and has shown themselves to be capable. We don't want to take any unnecessary risks here.

Decision-maker B is a 35-year old shopping center developer. This woman is self-made and pushes herself and everyone around her very hard. She is always looking for a better deal and a faster way to get things done. As she drives around in her BMW she has Bluetooth headsets on each ear and a fax machine in the back seat on which she is permanently making deals. What is her ideal firm like?

1. Fast.

2. Entrepreneurial. This firm thinks like she does and is always on the lookout for faster, cheaper ways to get the job done.

3. Out-of-the-box thinkers. This firm doesn't always play by the book because they know how to get around the red tape that can tie up an important project and its crucial funding.

Obviously, these two clients are worlds apart in their view of the ideal firm. And the firm that attempts to sell to these two clients using the same pitch, the same project sheets, and the same résumés will fail with both of them.

### Question #3: What are the reasons that this client might object to hiring you?

This question is an awkward one and could make you a little uncomfortable. If any of the participants in your meeting have strong egos, they should leave them parked at the door.

As good as you are, there are reasons or perceptions out there that influence clients to steer clear of you. Perhaps it's something straightforward, like the fact that your firm is too far from the project site or doesn't have a large enough staff to handle the project. It may be that you are perceived as being high-priced or too specialized or not specialized enough.

It may be something more difficult to deal with. Perhaps you have very little experience in this type of project. Maybe you have some recent black marks on your record because a couple of projects came in behind schedule or the quality of your contract documents was questioned by some contractors.

Your first step is to list all the possible objections, real or perceived, the client may have to hiring you.

### *Example*

1. Your firm only has 10 staff members and the client thinks the project needs more horsepower than that.

**BRAINSTORMING QUESTION #3**

What are the reasons that this client might object to hiring you?

As good as you are, there are reasons or perceptions out there that influence clients to steer clear of you. Perhaps it's something straightforward like the fact that your firm is too far from the project site or doesn't have a large enough staff to handle the project. It may be that you are perceived as being high priced or too specialized or not specialized enough.

1. _____
   True ☐   or   False ☐
   If true, what is the advantage?     _____
   If no advantage, what is the compensation _____
   Can we risk ignoring it?     Yes ☐   or   No ☐
   Is it a deal-breaker?     Yes ☐   or   No ☐

2. _____
   True ☐   or   False ☐
   If true, what is the advantage?     _____
   If no advantage, what is the compensation _____
   Can we risk ignoring it?     Yes ☐   or   No ☐
   Is it a deal-breaker?     Yes ☐   or   No ☐

3. _____
   True ☐   or   False ☐
   If true, what is the advantage?     _____
   If no advantage, what is the compensation _____
   Can we risk ignoring it?     Yes ☐   or   No ☐
   Is it a deal-breaker?     Yes ☐   or   No ☐

4. _____
   True ☐   or   False ☐
   If true, what is the advantage?     _____
   If no advantage, what is the compensation _____
   Can we risk ignoring it?     Yes ☐   or   No ☐
   Is it a deal-breaker?     Yes ☐   or   No ☐

Have you considered:

| | |
|---|---|
| Reputation | Past mistakes |
| Personality | Political affiliations |
| Past relationships | Design style |
| Firm size | Office location |
| Joint venture partners | Lack of experience |
| Professional fees | Focus of expertise |

Taboo subjects such as client prejudice

> When you have completed this form, hang it on the wall for reference during the preparation of the proposal and presentation.

2. Your firm is considered an expert in high-tech projects, but this project is focused in a very particular aspect of technology in which you have little experience.

3. Your office is located 150 miles from the project site.

4. Five years ago, one of your principals made a remark in a public meeting that offended the mayor, who is now on the board of directors of the client's company.

5. Six months ago, you got some bad press because the client was unable to obtain the rezoning they required and blamed you publicly for the failure.

Very often, the selection process is not a question of "who wins?" Instead it often comes down to "who's left standing at the end of an elimination process?" In a competition among virtual equals, your client will be looking for excuses to eliminate contenders. Any of the reasons shown above would be good enough to knock you off the list. If you head into the sales process without knowing about or being prepared to deal with these objections, you might as well not bother at all.

Now that you've identified all the major reasons why this client would *not* want to hire you, what can you do about it? The next step is to take each objection and analyze it by answering the following questions.

1. Is this objection true, or is it simply a perception on the part of the client?

   If it is simply a perception, your proposal must reveal the truth.

   **Example:** The client has heard that several of your recent projects went over budget and fell behind schedule. You must be prepared to show why that happened due to another party's action, such as how a client on one project significantly expanded the scope of the work.

2. If the objection is true, how can you show it to be an *advantage* to the client?

   **Example:** The client is concerned about the fact that your firm has a staff of only 10. Be prepared to explain that a small firm allows you the freedom to think and act like a SWAT team: you are small enough to move quickly and decisively on any issue. You are also free, when the need arises, to go out and find sub-consultants who are the tops in their field and to hand-pick the individuals who are best suited to make up the ideal team for the project. This is in direct contrast to those big firms who are stuck in their bureaucracy and who must use their in-house staff, even if they aren't the best suited for the task.

Conversely, if the concern be that your firm is too big, then explain that your large firm has all the needed resources under one roof. There is no situation that may arise on the project that your firm has not already handled. Additionally, if more resources or special expertise is needed, you simply have to pick up the intercom to access it.

(We marketers like to call that "spin"!)

3.  If you are unable to show the objection to be an advantage, what will you propose to offset it?

    **Example:** The client is concerned about the fact that your office is 150 miles from the project site. Admittedly, it's hard to show this to be an advantage, so be prepared to explain to the client that you have already arranged to lease office space directly across the street from the project for the duration of the job and staff it with the two key people who will be devoted full time to the project.

4.  If you are unable to show it to be an advantage or offer a way to accommodate the disadvantage, should you risk ignoring this objection and hope the client doesn't notice or hasn't had it brought to their attention? This is a very risky option and, by this time you may be getting desperate. However, you just might get lucky and have a client who doesn't put much merit in that particular aspect or think to ask about it.

5.  If you ignore the objection and the client *does* notice, will you immediately be knocked out of the competition? If the issue is indeed a killer, this is a very good time to revisit your go/no-go decision before you spend any more money on the proposal. Perhaps you have identified an issue that you hadn't noticed before. Better to cut bait and leave now rather than spend more money on the sales effort knowing it can't succeed.

Of course, you have to exercise a level of judgment as to whether you actually raise these issues in your business development effort or simply prepare yourself to address them if they come up. Some issues, such as the 150 mile distance from the project site, are so obvious that you can't escape them. In these cases, you should be proactive and head 'em off at the pass by dealing with it before the client has a chance to be concerned. In other issues, such as the one about firm size, it might be best not to mention the point unless the client brings it up. If that happens, you should be prepared with a suitable, confident and convincing answer to their concern.

Brainstorm your answers onto Form #3 and hang it on the wall.

### Question #4: Who will be competing against you on this project?

This question asks you to list the major competitors you will—or are likely to—face in competition for this project. If there are upwards of be 20 firms competing for the project, list only the top 5 that are likely to give you serious competition.

This, of course, will draw on the information in the dossier that you have prepared on your competitors in the previous chapter. By keeping up with the latest developments at your competitors" firms, you won't have any trouble identifying their strengths and weaknesses.

Using Form #4, for each competing firm list:

1.   The aspects of the firm that make them so good and likely to beat you
2.   The weaknesses which make them fall down and lose projects like this

Be honest in your evaluation of both strengths and weaknesses—they have plenty of both. Your corporate pride may make it too easy to criticize and say, "They can't do anything right." Obviously they can or they would not be considered competitors.

## Now what?

Now that you have answered all four questions you have some unexpected information that can help you wire yourself directly to the client's brain in your proposal and presentation effort. You have clearly described:

### 1. What the client wants to buy

The client doesn't want to buy design services, they want to buy smooth relations with the business district. They want to buy a short, untroubled, delay-free schedule. A bridge can be bought from many

**BRAINSTORMING QUESTION #4**

Who will you be competing against on this project?

Your competitors are pretty good. (That's why we call them 'competitors.') And on any given day they might beat you. Be honest in your evaluation of why they're so good and where they have chinks in their armor.

Competitor #1 _____

       Strength    _____
                   _____

       Weakness   _____
                   _____

Competitor #2 _____

       Strength    _____
                   _____

       Weakness   _____
                   _____

Competitor #3 _____

       Strength    _____
                   _____

       Weakness   _____
                   _____

Consider that a practice can have a positive or negative reputation for:

| | |
|---|---|
| Technical capability | Cost control |
| Reputation | Design talent |
| Political connections | Pricing |
| Past relationships | Experience profile |
| Political correctness | Perceived value |
| Past mistakes | Personality traits |
| Design style | Firm size |
| Office location | Joint venture partners |
| Professional fees | |

> When you have completed this form, hang it on the wall for reference during the preparation of the proposal and presentation.

sources. Only you can deliver trouble-free relations with the toll authority. Refer to these hot buttons throughout your proposal and presentation efforts to ensure the client sees your firm as the only viable solution to their real objectives.

### 2. Who the client wants to hire

You now know exactly who that decision maker wants to hire and you will set about to show that you are that firm. You will include nothing in your sales effort that does not correspond to any traits of the client's ideal firm because the checklist of traits you have created will now be used to describe your firm.

### 3. Why the client might hesitate to hire you.

The flaws you must correct or counter before the client will comfortably hire you are very clear now. Your sales effort will either address these issues head on or be fully prepared to show how they are non-issues. Your client's potential objections have been completely neutralized.

### 4. Why your competitor will win the project as well as why they might just fall flat on their faces.

Every coach will tell you that you must never go into a game without knowing the strengths and weaknesses of your opponent. Knowledge of your rivals' key weapons and the chinks in their armor can suggest powerful strategies that you can use to position yourself strongly, while at the same time counteracting their strengths.

## Building your game plan

Imagine for a moment that you've been assigned the task of selecting a design firm for an upcoming project that your company or government department is going to build. In front of you is a stack of 20 proposals, every one of them looks and reads the same, and you've got to narrow the pile down to 4 or 5 firms that will make the short list.

How will you go about doing that—narrowing the field to a few firms? What criteria will you use?

It's easy to sympathize with the plight of the evaluator who has to select 4 or 5 out of 20 firms that will then be subjected to a more thorough review. The exercise quickly becomes "How can we eliminate 15 of these contenders?"

Now, let's jump to the flip side of this situation. Yours is one of the proposals in the pile. Your firm is just one of a long list of firms vying for the project. What are *you* going to do make sure your firm is included when they narrow the field? What criteria will you *create* that will ensure your firm ends up in the short pile?

## Making the short list

To make the short list, you have two strategy options:

1.  Play it safe and avoid offending anyone who might give your firm a black mark. This is the defensive strategy.

2.  Grab their attention by the throat, throw them to the ground with your laser-focused response and take an aggressive approach that leaves them absolutely no choice but to include you on the short list. This is the offensive tactic.

Since every good coach knows the best defense is a good offense, we're going to use the second strategy to win this particular game.

Your aggressive game plan will use a three-prong strategy:

1.  It must be bold.
2.  It must differentiate you from your competition.
3.  It must be client-centered.

Let's look at each one.

## 1. Boldness

There is nothing easier in the A/E industry than to come in second in a project selection process. It must be easy because so many firms regularly accomplish it!

You never hear, "We came fifth!" All the time it's, "We came second." Or sometimes "We came a close second!" (As if that paid more than "regular" second!) The point is, in this business, you either win or you lose. There is no such thing as second place, just one winner, and a whole string of losers.

I believe very strongly that the riskiest thing a firm can do today is to be normal, predictable and "safe." Why is that risky? Because you risk looking exactly like every other firm with which you are competing. And that road leads to commodity pricing.

The upside is that the client is looking for a firm that is unique. There are hundreds of firms that can accomplish the work, but only one that has the unique talents and approaches of your firm. The business development effort is one of your prime opportunities to strut that uniqueness.

You're going to make your sales effort a clear, proud statement that your firm is *not like the rest*. Never aim to be average or adequate. Aim either to score a perfect 10, or to go down in flames and come dead last with a 0.

## 2. Differentiation

If all firms were identical, the services they sell would be commodities and clients would select exclusively on price.

Life would actually be much easier. You'd employ a room full of estimators who processed bid requests. They'd put together quotes—kind of like those Internet services for getting prices on car insurance or a vacation—and you'd win some projects and lose others.

But every firm is not identical. Your firm has significant value, both basic value and added value, to bring to your clients. You pride yourself on how you do your work, the unique approaches you use to solve your clients' challenges and the singular chemistry that defines your office.

If you're so different, why then do your business development, proposal and presentation efforts look and sound like those of every other firm's?

Think that your proposals are somehow different? Let's examine just one fragment of your sales effort. Pull out one of your recent proposals and see if you recognize some of these features:

- It's bound with a plastic comb or spiral binding.

- The title on the front cover is a direct re-statement of the project title given by the client in the RFP.

- The cover letter begins with a statement similar to: "We are pleased to have this opportunity to submit this proposal." Or "Thank you for the opportunity to submit this proposal."

- The relevant experience and résumé sections consist primarily of lists of projects you've done.

- The "Project Approach" section tells how your "team approach" will ensure the project's success.

These aren't features taken from *your* proposal. They are features found in practically every proposal ever written for the past 20 years! Talk about an industry stuck in a rut!

I believe that every proposal writer should be sentenced to 30 days of reviewing and evaluating other firms' proposals! It would underscore just how little difference there is between capture strategies today. By and large, if you remove the names and logos from the documents, there is virtually nothing to distinguish one from another.

You, however, have just decided that differentiation is a key to your future business development efforts and you want to learn everything you can about it.

There are four methods that your firm can use to differentiate itself:

1. Demonstrate some *unique* experience in the targeted project type. This is by far the most common, the most primitive, and the least effective means of distinguishing one's firm from the competition. Every significant competitor has experience that is equivalent to yours. If they didn't, they would not be a competitor. The most challenging aspect of this method is to show that your experience is unlike your competitors', that it is indeed *unique*. More often than not, the proposals I see simply say, "We did a project like this."

2. Show that the *process* you use to accomplish a client's goals is different and superior to that used by the competition. Today's client, concerned about quality and budget control, is sophisticated and vitally interested in the methods you use to achieve their objectives. Demonstration and explanation of your process also communicates competence and builds confidence. Letting the client see "behind the curtain" gives a sense of belonging to the inner circle and encourages a closer bond.

3. Prove that the *value* of your services is quantitatively better than those of your competition. This means you have to be able to measure and demonstrate improved efficiency, economy, or productivity in your client's organization as a result of your work. This is the most effective and meaningful means of differentiating. Most other industries have used this method

of differentiation for years (think about the comparison between two shirts, one washed in the featured brand and the
other in brand X), but it is almost never done in the design
industry. It's extremely difficult (although not impossible) and
it takes creativity and guts to step outside the norm. Can you
show, for example, that the long-term cost of operation and
maintenance of the facilities you design is lower than average?

4. Let every aspect of contact with your firm be an experience
   that is different from that of your competitors. This includes
   everything from the way you answer the phone to the way
   you manage projects to the way you conduct your business
   development and sales efforts. Your firm must look, feel, act
   and *be* different from all the others.

## 3. Client focus

Remember the important point we made in Chapter 2? We said that
human beings are egocentric. That is, everyone in the world shares the
same favorite subject: themselves.

When preparing and executing a capture plan, your firm is most comfortable talking and writing about your favorite subject—yourselves. But
when a client listens to and reads your stuff, they want to hear about
*their* favorite subject. The truth is, they really aren't interested in knowing about you, except as it affects them.

As the client reads through your proposal and listens to your presentation, they're asking themselves, "What's in this for me?" Yes, they want
to know about your experience, but they also want to know how it applies to them. How can you show what's in it for them?

Instead of providing a simple list of what you've done, you must *interpret* the list for them. You must tell them what you learned from the
experience and how it will save them money, reduce their schedule,
make them more popular with voters. . . . You get the picture.

Your sales effort must be, first and foremost, about your client, and it
must show them *directly* how they will be better off by hiring you.

But first, we need something to tie the entire business development effort together.

# Proposal themes

We've established that you are going to pursue an aggressive game plan using a three-prong strategy of boldness, differentiation and client focus. You will give consistency and unity to this three-pronged strategy by incorporating targeted, client-centered themes throughout your business development and sales effort.

Where can you find these themes?

The themes you will incorporate are the ones you identified in the brainstorming session earlier in this chapter. Remember that the four brainstorming questions you posed produced some remarkable information.

You clearly described:

1. **What the client wants to buy.** The hot buttons that you identified now become themes that are woven throughout your sales effort. This will let the client clearly see their own objectives being accomplished through your proposal and presentation.

2. **Who the client wants to hire.** The traits of the ideal firm will also become themes that appear again and again through your business development. These will confirm in the client's mind that you are that firm of their dreams.

3. **Why the client might hesitate to hire you.** Armed with this valuable information, you will now tackle and dispel these issues throughout your sales effort in order to ease their mind and raise the client's comfort level.

4. **The strengths and weaknesses of your competitors.** While you will never name names, you will certainly use this knowledge to reinforce your position and, perhaps, plant a few seeds of doubt that might get the client to pay extra-critical attention to some weaknesses on the part of your competition.

These items will now serve as the themes that occur in every facet of your business development effort. You've crawled inside your client's head and seen how things look from their point of view. Now you'll learn how to incorporate them into your proposal and presentation efforts.

# Part 2
# Proposals and Presentations

# Introduction

## It's not just about qualifications

Your proposal is not just a technical document conveying data. It has to persuade, assure, convince, comfort, and win over a client who is about to put a great deal of money in your hands. Your proposal is not only about qualifications. It's a personal message.

If we're going to think of that boring, old proposal in these terms, we're going to have to rethink how the proposal is organized. Here is an excerpt from an actual RFP issued by a municipal client looking to retain design services. It describes what the city would like to see in the proposal responses.

*The proposal shall include*

1. *Size and make-up of the firm*
2. *Names and résumés of personnel to be assigned to the project*
3. *A list of related projects and references*
4. *A list of other disciplines that would be included in the proposal*
5. *Previous experience with similar projects*
6. *Proven ability to adhere to schedules and budgets, within particular emphasis on design consulting*
7. *A description of the methodology and procedures to be used for the total scope of this project. (i.e., concept phase, design phase, public input phases)*
8. *Fees disbursement and hourly charge-out rates for the concept design phase*

As we pointed out in Chapter 3, clients are as bad at writing RFPs as we are at writing the proposals that respond to them. Taken at face value, the above list becomes a handy checklist that can be given to a marketing coordinator, assembled and submitted to the client for review. It would be filled with boilerplate and generic answers that are copied from the answers given in previous proposals to other clients.

But this approach entirely misses the point!

Instead of taking a checklist approach to your proposal, I've been suggesting that you need to crawl inside the client's head and discover what it is they are actually looking for. Instead of taking a checklist approach, read the list above again and realize that what it actually says is:

*The Proposal Shall Include:*

*Sufficient information, presented in a concise, easy-to-access and persuasive manner to convince the selection committee to hire you and not someone else.*

Let's learn how to provide exactly that.

# 7

# First Impressions

## Scary story #1:

Some years ago I was facilitating a proposal-writing workshop with about 20 CEOs of design and construction firms. I had a stack of proposals and I asked the group to think of themselves as a client selection panel. Their job was to review the proposals and reduce the large pile to two smaller ones: the short list and the rejects.

We passed out the proposals and these high-ranking executives dove into them. What these CEOs did not know was that I was timing how long they took to make that initial decision about "Pile A" or "Pile B." The average time spent with each proposal before making that initial, crucial decision was 18 seconds.

Eighteen seconds! It takes longer than that to brush your teeth! And yet these highly skilled executives were willing to make important decisions based on the information they could assimilate in that incredibly short time.

## Scary story #2:

More recently I had occasion to be at the Naval Facilities Command in Norfolk, Virginia, where I was meeting with one of the Navy's contracting officers. She related how she had received 40 proposals in response to an RFP. Lacking the time to review them all she instructed, her assistant to line all the proposals up, leaning on the ledge below the white boards in the conference room. She then proceeded to walk into the room and, from a distance of 10 feet, select the 12 proposals she would review in detail.

All that incredibly detailed information you agonized over was never even seen. Kinda hurts, don't it?

On what were the executives and the contracting officer making the decisions? Nothing more than first impressions! As a result, I long ago determined that in order to wire your firm straight into your client's brain, you must think in terms of there being three—and only—three sections in a good proposal:

- The "First Impressions" section
- The "What We're Going to Do for You" section
- The "Who We Are" section

Of course you can't think of these three categories as you would normal sections separated by tabbed dividers. Instead, think of them as three critical messages that have to be delivered to your client, sometimes subliminally. Often these three messages will be intermingled with each other and spread throughout the proposal in the tabbed sections that the client has requested. But I encourage you to think of the how content you're preparing fits into these three sections. As you write, recast the standard, traditional proposal sections into this new context. At all times, imagine yourself as the client, having to review and evaluate the proposal.

Let's look at each of these in turn.

## First impressions

Yes, we do judge books by their covers.

Based on many scary experiences, I have concluded that the first and most important section of any proposal is what we'll call the First Impressions Section. It lasts 18 seconds, during which you have to grab their attention and get them to be sufficiently interested in what you're showing, that you make it to the short list.

Have you ever thought about how your potential client actually reviews your proposal? By this I mean the physical process of looking at it for the first time? It goes something like this: Your client holds the proposal in one hand and flips through it with the other thumb, starting from the back and moving to the front. As he does this he's observing how the pages are laid out, the kind of paper that it's printed on and any interesting graphics that might be included. Then he flips to the front and finds the cover letter. He begins to scan the letter and if the 18-second clock expires and he has still not seen anything that he thinks deserves further consideration, your proposal goes into the reject pile.

Use the First Impressions section to maximize the communication of information in the available period of time. You will have to learn how to communicate key information very, very quickly, because, if you don't do that, all the good stuff that's there in the middle of page 12 will never be seen.

The First Impressions section is intended to make an instant and significant impact, and it consists of:

- The cover and binding
- The title
- The page design, paper, and fonts you've used
- The cover letter you have written

## An intriguing cover story

The cover of your proposal is like the packaging a retailer uses to market its products. Think about the three different shopping bags you get shopping at Wal-Mart, Macy's, and Saks Fifth Avenue. Each bag tells a very different story about the store, the quality of the products it sells, and the type of customer it hopes to attract.

You never hear Saks' customers complaining about the cost of the fancy shopping bag or the salary of the uniformed doorman as they pull up on Wilshire Boulevard. But they know perfectly well those costs are added to the price of the products they buy. Nor do you hear Wal-Mart customers asking to have a doorman or more up-scale store fixtures. They also know these costs would add to the overhead of the store and passed on to them.

I once saw a proposal submitted to a developer in Chicago by a design/build team of architects and contractors. The project was a very high-end condominium project, the sort for which you pay $3 million for a two-bedroom unit. The proposal document was hardbound in black leather with gold leaf lettering on the front cover! It even smelled rich! Any client picking up that document would immediately know that the design/build team had completely understood the nature of the project.

Don't get me wrong. The public works director reviewing your proposal to conduct smoke tests on his sanitary sewer system would not appreciate the gesture!

The point is that you have choices. You can choose an appropriate cover design to instantly demonstrate that you grasp an important aspect of the client's project. Make the appropriate choice based on what you know of the client and the project from your research, your brainstorming and your game plan.

## An eye-catching title

The titles of most proposals are as dull as grey paint. Why not jazz things up a little? A good title is like a headline in a newspaper article: it grabs your attention and hints at what you can expect to discover.

If the schedule is going to be a big deal on your project, refer to on-time delivery in the title. If there is a significant technical challenge on the project, work your solution into the title and splash it on the cover. Here are some examples based on an actual RFP for A/E services for a Federal correctional facility in Virginia. The RFP from the client was titled:

**Request for Proposal for Architect/Engineering Services**
**Federal Correctional Facilities**
**Lee County, Virginia**
**SOL RFP X00-0264**
**Federal Bureau of Prisons**

The predictable, traditional reaction would be to title the proposal:

**Response to Request for Proposal for Architect/Engineering Services**
**Federal Correctional Facilities**
**Lee County, Virginia**
**SOL RFP X00-0264**
**Federal Bureau of Prisons**

Not only is this boring and unimaginative, it fails to tell the client anything they don't already know. It doesn't reflect any of the unique aspects of your firm and it doesn't respond to any of the issues that the project may face. Lastly, it fails to differentiate you from any competitor because you can guarantee they will all use the same title. Surely you can do better than this.

Using the headline idea, if a major hot button on the project is schedule, why not try:

**Virginia Prison Locked Up in 28 Months**

If the big challenge is cost control you could use:

### Under Lock, Key, and Budget in Virginia

If relations with the local community are a big issue:

### Federal Correctional Facilities: Building Community Ties

Look to the type of project to give you ideas about an innovative title:

A renovation project for a corporate client:

### Updating Your Investment in the Phoenix Building

A road reconstruction for a municipality:

### Keeping the Traffic Flowing at Maple and Elm Streets

A student housing center:

### Housing Our Future Leaders at Auburn College

Titles like these not only set you apart from everyone else; they intrigue and delight the reader. They give some hint about the contents of the proposal and they cause the client to forget about their 18-second clock!

## Appropriate and attractive covers and bindings

Choosing an attractive and appropriate binding for your proposal tells the client that you care enough to think about packaging it in something other than the same old predictable thing. There are plenty of options available, so why not get creative?

### Plastic comb

Used for far too many proposals. It looks cheap and is cheap. It's also old. While some firms "customize" the binding by having their name printed on the spine, it doesn't remove the low-cost impact.

### Plastic spiral

Still low end, but a step up from comb binding.

### Metal wire

Metal wire binding is inexpensive but more classy than plastic.

### 3-ring binder

Binders can look very smart, especially the type with a clear plastic cover. This allows you to create a custom cover and make each proposal look different. Another choice is to have a set of binders custom silk-screened and used for all proposals. Binders are available in a variety of qualities.

### Hard covers

There are many forms of binding available today that make it easy to put together professional-looking "books" quickly and at low cost. At the same time, you can go as far as you want with hard covers. I've seen leather, wood, stainless steel and hand-made paper that was hand-laced with natural vines and twigs. You name the material and there probably is a project for which it would be a suitable binding material. Just make sure it matches the client's view of the project.

### Totally customized

I've seen proposal covers that had been created from tree bark, sewn by hand, welded from metal, crafted from cork board and a whole host of other, incredibly creative options. In each case, the cover and binding was an imaginative and customized response to that particular client's needs and situation. Get creative!

## An attractive page design

The information you need to convey to your client can be obscured, if not completely hidden, by a poorly designed page. It is a mistake to assume that since the words are on the page, the reader will find, read, and understand them. A well-designed page will aid dramatically in prioritizing and communicating the information it holds.

There are a few simple rules that will make you a master page designer.

1. Find a page design that is attractive, simple and effective and stick with it. Don't continually mess around with alternative page layouts. It wastes your time and doesn't substantially improve your proposals.

2. Separate the discrete pieces of information in your proposal into separate blocks of text on the page. Allow enough space between distinct thoughts to allow the readers eyes to rest and assimilate what you've just said. If the thought is important enough, start a new page with a new heading.

3.  Use an invisible grid to organize your layout so each page looks similar to the others. If all the elements on each page (titles, graphics, text, pictures) conform to the grid you will have achieved a uniform, consistent look throughout the entire proposal.

If you are stuck for ideas, look in books and magazines and copy the layouts of the pages you find attractive. Measure the margins and the spaces between columns of text and duplicate it in your proposal. If you find it appealing, your clients likely will as well.

Better yet, retain the services of a professional graphic designer to prepare a proposal template for you. Have them design the location of text and picture blocks, suggest white space areas and choose fonts and color schemes. Then stick to it. Don't try to tweak it. Remember: you're a professional engineer or architect. You don't expect people to start "tweaking" your bridge or building designs. You know what you're doing and you expect your clients to trust you. So does the graphic designer.

## A nice piece of paper

Your choices in paper stock range all the way from handmade, recycled sheets with chunks of wood floating around in it, to high gloss, high tech, metallic paper. There are also pre-printed sheets that can run through your laser printer for a custom look at low cost.

These papers are also easy to find and obtain. There are numerous mail order paper companies who will send you 5 or 5,000 sheets, with matching covers, envelopes, and note cards, depending on what you want. You no longer have any excuse for submitting a boring document on 20-pound white bond paper.

However, just because these papers are available does not mean you should automatically use them. Just as you will choose a cover and binding appropriate to the project and the client, you should choose paper stock that sends the same, consistent message.

If the project is high-class and elegant, select something refined. If it's an environmental job, use a recycled paper. If the culture of the organization you are submitting your proposal to is creative and upbeat, select a paper stock that reinforces that message.

There are even times when the best choice is your own office stationery. But don't assume that using stationery is appropriate for every proposal.

## Fonts

Today there are thousands of fonts to choose from and the selection can be overwhelming to the untrained eye. Here's an easy rule to remember: Most of the fonts that came loaded on your computer should never be used in your proposals, mainly because they are too "cute" or unusual.

There are two major font groups, serif and sans serif. Serif refers to any font in which the letters have the small strokes at their ends. It should almost always be used for blocks of text because that little stroke actually allows the eye to move smoothly from one letter and word to the next. Sans Serif refers to those fonts that don't have the strokes. They can provide a more "contemporary" look but make reading blocks of text more difficult. They should be reserved for headings and titles.

Serif fonts which you should commonly use include:

Times
Palatino
New Century Schoolbook

Sans serif fonts that are useful include:

Helvetica
Gill Sans
Futura

Keep your selection of fonts to a minimum to avoid a busy look to your page. Your proposal can achieve all the highlighting and emphasis necessary by choosing one serif and one sans serif font and varying size, emphasis, and capitalization.

ALL CAPITALS
SMALL CAPITALS
**Bold**
*Italic*

With the technology we have available, font selection is far too easy and, with inexperienced users, the results are often garish. It will be a good return on your investment to engage a professional graphic designer to suggest some font families that will make your proposals elegant and eye-pleasing.

## An accessible writing style

*"I don't know the rules of grammar. . . . If you're trying to persuade people to do something, or buy something, it seems to me you should use their language, the language they use every day, the language in which they think. We try to write in the vernacular."*

David Ogilvy

If your primary goal in a proposal is to persuade the client—we talked about the various aspects of persuasion in Chapter 1—then you need to use all the tools at our disposal to accomplish that goal. One of the most important is to make the content of your proposal easily accessible and understood. Too many technical professionals have been trained in technical writing and use that style in their proposals.

While technical writing may be accurate, it's crushingly boring to read. You want to generate excitement and enthusiasm on the part of your client. And that doesn't happen from perusing something that reads like a specification.

Instead, you want to write in a more comfortable, easy-going style. One of the tests you can use to check your writing style is read a passage that you've written out loud to yourself. Then ask, "Does this sound like me talking?" If it sounds a little too stiff and formal, rewrite it and relax your writing style. Here is a sample of "before" and "after" proposals, in which the writing style has been made much more relaxed and therefore easier to read.

### Before: Accurate, yet crushingly dull

Preconstruction Services
During the preconstruction phase Acme Construction shall:

- Develop detailed estimates of costs of materials, equipment and labor
- Review facility life cycle costing implications
- Conduct value analysis and value engineering
- Conduct a constructability review
- Review and finalize schedule
- Assemble and coordinate Bid Packages
- Identify and prequalify subcontractors and suppliers

**After: Far more interesting and engaging, yet still accurate**

During preconstruction we will:

- Estimate the detailed costs of materials, equipment and labor. Then we have to live and die with our estimates.

- Examine the total cost of ownership that you will incur with your facility to ensure a small savings now doesn't become a maintenance nightmare later.

- Conduct a detailed value analysis to make sure the materials and equipment specified are those that give you the best value for your construction dollar.

- Walk through the entire construction process to uncover any constructability challenges and solve them now before the pricey crane is brought on site.

- Review the schedule in fine detail to find the fastest possible way to get this facility completed and get your revenue flowing.

- Assemble the individual bid packages to ensure 100 percent coverage but avoid costly overlaps, confusion and wasted time and money.

- Identify and prequalify those subcontractors and suppliers who are best suited to contribute to the success of this project.

With the consequences of getting it wrong so critical, it will be reassuring for you to have Acme Construction's experienced Preconstruction Team, with our wealth of knowledge and lessons-learned, assembling the framework for a successful [your project name here] project.

# A unique cover letter

The cover letter you write can significantly influence your client's initial reaction to your proposal. It is one of the first items the client will read in the crucial early seconds of their review and it plays an important role in forming their first impressions.

Most firms treat it as a simple transmittal letter and fill it with trite, meaningless statements such as "We are pleased to submit this proposal," or "We are uniquely qualified," or "If you have any questions, please call." These sentences appear in virtually every proposal and only serve to reinforce the client's impression that all firms are the same. In contrast, your objective should be to do everything possible to underscore the differences between you and everyone else.

Your cover letter ought to be so powerful that your client could make up his or her mind by reading it alone. Therefore, the letter ought to be comprehensive enough to persuade them to put you on the short list. But it also has to be short enough to be quickly scanned and understood. Think of the cover letter as a mini-executive summary and you'll be well on your way to success.

Here's how to do it. Let's say you are proposing design services for a new medical center and your brainstorming session has resulted in the following issues in response to the four questions:

**Hot buttons**

- Completing the project within 18 months
- Maintaining positive community relations
- Maintaining ongoing operations during construction
- Control over a very tight budget

**Ideal firm**

- Located within 20 minutes of the project
- Willing to accept input of Board of Directors and doctors
- Full-service firm with all in-house disciplines
- Project manager who has extensive medical center experience

**Objections to your firm**

- Located 100 miles away from the project                          (true)
- Lacks in-house engineering staff                                 (true)
- Project manager has little medical center experience     (false)
- Not the firm we've always worked with                            (true)

**Competition**

| Acme Architects | + high quality contract documents<br>– poor reputation for budget control |
| Ace Architects | + strong project management capability<br>– last project resulted in poor client relations |
| Long & Short A/E | + worked with client before<br>– high priced |

Using these key issues as an outline, your cover letter can address the project and the client's specific issues like this:

*Dr. Tom Brown*
*Western Medical Center*
*123 State Street*
*Yourtown, ST 12345*

*Re: Strong staff and community relations for the project*

*Dear Dr. Brown:*

*The Western Medical Center's new Inpatient Pediatric project is a wonderful opportunity for the hospital to reinforce its strong community ties and staff relationships. By emphasizing the input of your Board and doctors, we fully expect that your aggressive 18-month schedule can be met within budget.*

*Smith and Jones has been studying this project extensively and has developed a unique scheduling process that will ensure the smooth operation of the rest of your facility during construction. To make the process as smooth as possible, we have already mapped out a schedule of community information meetings to invite comments from the surrounding neighborhood.*

*In addition, you can look forward to:*

- *A thoughtful and coordinated process for input by Board and staff members (see page 12)*
- *A project manager with a remarkable talent for smooth community relations (page 8)*
- *A peaceful night's sleep with the knowledge that the budget is well under control (see page 4)*

*Although you have not had the opportunity to work with Smith and Jones previously, many of your peers have found the experience economical, efficient, professional, and downright pleasant! We invite you to review their comments, which can be found throughout this proposal. In addition, working with Smith and Jones on this project will give you the opportunity to compare the levels of service, responsiveness, quality, and economy you have received from other firms.*

*I will contact you during the next week to clarify any questions you may have regarding our approach to the project. In the meantime, we are continuing to review the specifics of this project and prepare for kickoff.*

*Yours frugally,*

*Smith and Jones, Inc.*
*John J. Smith*

*PS: We are looking forward to demonstrating our unique cost control process at the interview.*

Obviously this entire letter was built around the issues that are important to the client. As a result, it addresses the client's concerns specifically and avoids those "mom-and-apple-pie" statements used by everyone else.

You can see that the subject of this letter is no longer your firm. It has shifted to the client and their project. This subtle but important shift takes us back to Chapter 6, where our 3-pronged capture strategy involves a strong client focus and an incorporation of proposal "themes." With the client as the main subject and a strong emphasis on the benefits that are in it for them, the likelihood that they will read and be intrigued by your letter is very high indeed.

You will also notice some other intriguing features of the letter that are designed to catch a client's eye and entice them to read further. The technique of giving each bullet point a page reference allows a reader who is intrigued by that issue to go straight to the relevant page in the proposal. Instead of reading one page at a time, they can focus on the highlights of their particular issue.

The PS is another feature that is guaranteed to be read. Even if they only skim your letter, the client will always stop to read the PS. Use it to hit another hot button that provokes them to keep reading or to find out more about you.

Human nature being what it is, it's not surprising that the majority of selection committee participants admit they have significantly made up their minds within the first seconds or minutes of picking up a proposal. It is in your best interest, then, to make the most of this opportunity by making a memorable first impression that puts you into an entirely different category from the rest of your competitors.

# 8

# What We'll Do For You

Imagine this bizarre scenario:

You are about to take the major step of constructing a new home. You and your spouse are interviewing builders and hoping to select one that will create your dream home. Each builder takes you on a wonderful tour of projects they have and describe in detail how happy each of their previous customers is with their new home.

But when you ask about the home they will build for you, they never seem to come up with anything better than generic statements about how it will be a "quality home" made with "the best materials." It's unlikely that you'd be willing to hire any of these builders because they either refuse or are unable to see the world from your point of view and get specific about the solution that *you* are seeking.

This is the situation in which many clients of design professionals find themselves. When it comes right down to it, a client doesn't much care what you've done for someone else. They are first and foremost concerned with what you're going to do for them. Your past experience and credentials are only important because they *suggest* what you are likely to do now.

Clients are happy to hear about your experience but, sooner or later, they want you to get specific about what you can do for them. The "What We're Going to Do for You" section of your proposal gives your client a clear idea of exactly what they are buying.

There are usually (although not always) three major components in this section:

1. A Statement of Understanding
2. The Scope of Work
3. Your Approach to the Project

## Statement of understanding

This is your opportunity to set your firm apart from the crowd by demonstrating your knowledge of the client's needs and expectations. To do this successfully, you've got to show the real insight you've gained into the situation through your research and brainstorming. It's no good to simply repeat the statements that were made in the RFP.

Here's a good example:

An actual RFP read, in part, as follows:

> *The City intends to commission the services of a qualified A/E firm to develop concept plans for the overall design of a new aquatic center and recreation facility to be placed before the public at a referendum in November.*

The predictable response in a Statement of Understanding would be to write something like:

> *Smith and Jones understands that the City requires a qualified A/E firm to develop concept plans for the overall design of a new aquatic center and recreation facility. In addition, these plans will be used to present the proposed aquatic center to the public in a referendum in November.*

As uninspiring as this is, I've seen far too many proposals with statements that are equally unimaginative.

Your job is to show the client that you *truly* understand the challenge they face and that your services will actually provide a solution to their problem. Perhaps your response could sound more like this:

> *At Smith and Jones we have spent considerable time investigating the details and circumstances surrounding the new aquatic center and recreation facility. With the level of public support for this project currently at about 50/50, we know that not only will the City need an attractive and functional design, you will require a compelling and enthusiastic presentation at the public meeting prior to the referendum in November. We intend to work with both your staff and with City Council members in order to make the design work together with public opinion so this project can be a success.*

A statement like this demonstrates that you have insight beyond a mere checklist of things to be done. You are willing to become an active team member who not only provides design and technical expertise, but also contributes to the solution of the "big picture."

When you write a Statement of Understanding, avoid generic statements that are applicable in any situation—they will come off sounding like boilerplate. A statement such as this:

> *We understand this project must meet your program requirements while maintaining both schedule and budget.*

is trite, obvious and absolutely meaningless. Every project has this requirement. Show that you've done your homework by taking the client's issues and adding value, interpretation and insight . . . and do it in a short, concise statement.

# Scope of services

Your statement of scope needs to be a specific listing of what the client can expect to receive in exchange for their money and their trust in you.

One of the most effective ways of delineating your services is through a Work Breakdown Structure (WBS). A WBS allows you to organize a large complex undertaking such as a project and break it down into logical work packages. It also lends itself well to diagram form, simplifying your task of communicating a complex scope.

A work breakdown structure separates the project into its component parts, each of which can be seen as a mini-project on its own. A simple diagram explains the concept.

The beauty of the WBS is not simply its ability to communicate scope to a client. It helps you identify the tasks that will be necessary to complete a project. By beginning with a simple description of the overall project and working systematically through the job, you can develop a thorough listing of the tasks involved.

The WBS is also a wonderful aid for discussions with your client. It clearly identifies all the tasks that are necessary for completion of the project. Should the client wish to cut costs, they can easily see the implications of removing one task or another.

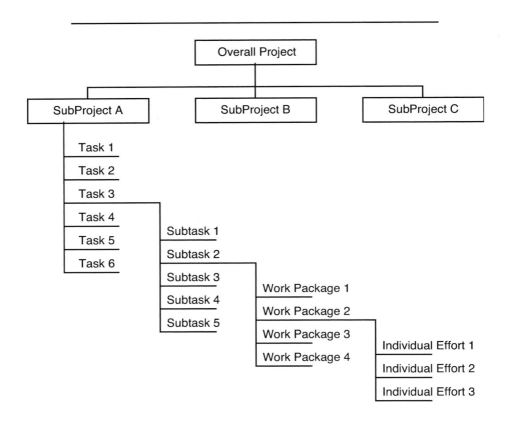

It's also useful in discussions regarding who will be responsible for which tasks. By laying them out in the WBS, you can conveniently assign responsibility to yourself, a subconsultant or the client. This can form the basis of project planning discussions and contract negotiations.

Whether or not you use a Work Breakdown Structure, your scope of services should essentially be a series of five lists:

**1. What are the services to be included?** This is done best with a detailed listing or the Work Breakdown Structure.

**2. What are the services that are specifically excluded?** Those items that are not included should be spelled out in detail. For example:

*The study will make use of available data, visual observations and interviews with end users. It will not include extensive research into the detailed system parameters, load calculations or drawing updates.*

**3. What are the services that are optionally available?** Services or approaches that are outside the scope of work need to be identified and offered to the client as choices.

*At your discretion, the City may choose for us to pursue an alternate design approach which our visual inspection of the project site has identified. We feel this alternate design approach can provide significant savings in long term operating costs but could increase initial construction costs by as much as five percent.*

**4. What are the services that will be provided at no charge?** Everybody likes free stuff. So why not provide your client with free services? Before you get up in arms about the ethics of providing free professional services, let's make sure we understand the definition of "free."

*"Free" means the charge is not represented as a line item on your bill.*

The mints on the pillow at the Ritz-Carlton are "free." The first three years of scheduled maintenance on your new BMW are also "free." What might you include as free when providing your services? How about:

*The following services will be provided at no charge:*

- *The first five client-initiated change orders*
- *Rendering for use by your Marketing Department*
- *Representation at two public meetings*
- *Post-completion inspection at 6 months after start-up*

By offering these small items at no charge, you increase the perceived value of the overall service you provide.

**5. The set of deliverables the client can expect upon completion.** This should be in the form of a detailed list to protect you down the road from assumptions. For example:

*The deliverables from this project will be:*

1. *Written project plan presented at the project kickoff meeting*

2. *Development and maintenance of a project schedule*

3. *A written description of the construction guidelines compatible with the technology to be installed*

4. *Drawings of cable and terminal installations*

5. *Requirements for installation of cable and terminals*

6. *Written cable and terminal testing requirements*

7. *Detailed cable and terminal specifications*

8. *RFP and addenda for supply of cable and terminals*

9. *Recommendation of cable and terminal contractor*

10. *Written requirements for documentation of cable and terminal installation including cable records, testing and as-built drawings*

## Project approach

Unlike the Scope of Services that details *what* you are going to do, the Project Approach defines *how* you intend to go about the project. In discussions with your client, this is a wonderful opportunity to differentiate your firm from another by emphasizing you added value.

How will you tackle this project differently than you handled the last one? What's different about the project and your firm that requires a different and presumably better approach? What is it about this client and their situation that calls for changes or supplements to previous approaches?

Keep in mind that at all times you are attempting to differentiate yourself from your competitors. And trust me, if you tell your client that their project is exactly the same as all the others you've done, it might be the truth but it's not going to go over well.

There are often project areas where a unique approach may be critical. For example:

1. Should you invite your client to become involved in the design, perhaps through a *charette* or public input process?

2. Is there a proprietary process owned by you or the client that should be used? One construction company has developed and trademarked a process by which they calculate the total cost of facility ownership under various value-engineering scenarios.

3. Could an alternative approach to project sequencing ease the ability to maintain ongoing operations through the construction process?

There are many areas where your unique approach can provide a competitive edge and an advantage on the project.

- Scheduling
- Subcontracting and subconsulting
- Quality control and quality assurance
- Public input
- Permitting
- Value engineering
- Designer-contractor relations

Here is an example of an approach statement regarding the environmental permitting process. Notice how the statements are very specific. The client reading this can envision this process unfolding on their project. At the same time, they are getting the sense that this team has been down this road before.

> *There are two key elements to smooth and efficient environmental permitting. First, have a good project! If the project is well designed, makes a real attempt to minimize environmental impact (or, better yet, effects a positive change), and is within all of the agency's rules and guidelines, then there will be very few roadblocks that can delay or derail the review process. Second, good communication with the regulatory staff allows them to become familiar with the project before they actually review it, highlights the benefits of the project, minimizes potential confusion and provides the staff with a comfort level about the integrity of the design team and, by extension, the design itself.*
>
> *We would accomplish these two important goals by first integrating the environmental permitting team into the design effort so that they can be providing feedback and suggestions that will help keep the design within regulatory restrictions and add elements that will help regulators see the overall environmental benefits of the project. Second, we will keep in constant communication with regulatory staff to ensure that they are up-to-date with their understanding of the project and that they have everything they need to efficiently review the project.*

Here is another example of a well-structured approach statement. As you can see, this narrative also helps define the limits of the scope of work.

*Approach to the work*

*This is how we intend to approach the Long Island Road Interpretive Report. Of course, all work will conform with the guidelines set out by the State Historical Society and to the Secretary of the Interior's Standards for Identification and Evaluation of Historic Properties.*

*1. Project coordination*

*Our architectural history staff will meet with the State DOT to discuss the project schedule and objectives. We'll be looking for their approval of the schedule and proposed activities before any work gets under way. We will also meet with the archeological staff of the Valley Archaeology Center to coordinate the efforts on this project.*

*2. Background research*

*We will research the relevant historic and architectural contexts of the communities and resources along the Long Island Road. Sufficient information will be gathered to develop historic themes within the project area. Collections that will be consulted include local and county histories, historic photographs, newspapers and city directories; archival holdings of the State Historical Society's Historic Preservation Division; collections of local historical societies and organizations and collections of local public libraries within the project area.*

*3. Two public meetings*

*Two initial meetings will be held to introduce the project, the Project Manager and the team to the public. A member of the archeological staff will attend one of these two meetings. We will use visual displays to illustrate the goals of the project for the interested citizens. Public questions and comments will be addressed.*

# Hero stories

Your Project Approach section can also benefit from "hero stories" which describe how you have used unique methods in the past with positive results. Success stories are an enormously effective tool in persuading a client to choose your firm and we'll discuss them in greater detail in the next chapter.

The following story gave the client a real insight into the firm's approach and helped a large construction company win a prestigious project in downtown Washington, D.C.

> When we renovated six floors of the historic bank facility on Pennsylvania Avenue, the greatest challenge was to renovate the first floor banking hall while maintaining full banking services. With careful staging, night shifts for the dirty work and continuous clean-up operations, such as we intend to use on your project, we kept every customer clean, protected and happy as we reworked the marble teller counters to their original, 1920 configuration.

## Defining the client's responsibilities

Something that is often overlooked in the business development and proposal process is to clearly define the roles of each player. Since you won't be able to do the work effectively without input and contribution from the client, your project approach statements should also spell out what you need and expect from them. Here's an example that shows how you can detail this in your proposal.

*Acme Corporation's responsibilities*

*We all want this project to flow as smoothly and efficiently as possible. To accomplish that, Acme must be an active participant in the process. Among your major responsibilities will be:*

1. *Providing a single project coordinator who is dedicated to the successful completion of this job*

2. *Providing complete and accurate documentation of the existing systems and services in the facility*

3. *Making timely decisions consistent with the schedule we have prepared to allow our work and the work of other consultants and contractors to stay on schedule*

4. *Keeping us informed of any physical, organizational or other changes during the course of the project that might influence the outcome of the project.*

*In short, this project must be a collaborative effort between the Acme Corporation and Smith and Jones Engineers.*

Statements like this make it clear that you have not only thought the project through and identified areas where glitches may occur, you have also taken a leadership position in coordinating the effort that will be needed. This builds confidence on the part of a client who is looking for a consultant who will come in, take charge, and make the problem go away.

At this point, it's worthwhile to think back to Chapter 2, when we recognized that your job is to persuade your client to change his or her mind. Hero stories and detailed descriptions of the approach you intend to take allow the client to mentally visualize your firm doing the work. They can begin to picture you running the meetings, negotiating with the Public Works Department and walking the site with the contractor. The more stories you tell and the more specific you are, the clearer that picture becomes.

By painting a mental picture of you actually working on their project, you will have gone a long way towards persuading them to hire you and not someone else.

# 9
# Who We Are

Let's go back to the beginning of our discussion about proposals and review the list of requirements that the client included in their RFP.

*The proposal shall include*

1. *Size and make-up of the firm*
2. *Names and résumés of personnel to be assigned to the project*
3. *A list of related projects and references*
4. *A list of other disciplines that would be included in the proposal*
5. *Previous experience with similar projects*
6. *Proven ability to adhere to schedules and budgets, within particular emphasis on design consulting*
7. *A description of the methodology and procedures to be used for the total scope of this project. (i.e., concept phase, design phase, public input phases)*
8. *Fees disbursement and hourly charge-out rates for the concept design phase*

Of the eight items on the list, five ask about your firm, your capabilities and the team you intend to use.

In order to be comfortable in their decision, your client must develop a level of trust in your ability to deliver what you promise. We discussed this at length in Chapters 3 and 4. Recall that, since you're not selling cars that can be taken for a test drive and objectively compared, the client has no option but to look at your history and past performance as an indicator of how you're likely to perform on their project.

The Who We Are section is designed to reduce or eliminate the client's sense of risk when hiring you by establishing and reinforcing your capability to execute the project at hand.

This section might typically include:

- Relevant experience
- Personal profiles
- Firm and team profiles
- Organization charts
- References
- Testimonials

Let's look at ways in which these familiar items can be rebuilt to gain access to the inner workings of your client's decision making process.

## Relevant experience

In my brief moments of cynicism, I find myself referring to the proposal process for most projects as The Battle of the Lists. Proposals are usually introduced by a low-impact cover letter indicating that the firm has lots of relevant experience. The proposal then goes on to list the projects the firm has done. These projects are listed in many areas, including résumés, approach statements, experience, and other places, too. The lists carefully enumerate all the projects that the firm has done, giving the project name, the client, the completion date, and usually the construction cost.

Unfortunately, these lists do little or nothing to show the *value* that you brought to a client's project or the value that you will bring to this one. Take, for example, the following list of housing projects, which was taken from a typical proposal (the project names have been changed).

**Relevant experience**

*Golden Age Retirement Village*
*    101 elderly units and community building*
*    Three stories*
*    Construction costs: $3,233,500*

*Crawford Towers*
*    150 elderly units*
*    Five stories*
*    Construction cost: $3,688,000*

*Brighton High-rise for the Elderly*
    *110 elderly units*
    *10 stories*
    *Construction cost: $2,897,000*

*Conway Terrace*
    *248 units (195 new and 53 rehab.)*
    *Three stories and two stories*
    *Construction cost: $4,135,000*

Lists like this are everywhere and they do you little or no good as you attempt to distinguish yourself from your competitors. Why are lists of this sort so ineffective as marketing tools? Because your competitor has submitted a proposal that contains a list that looks almost identical. Here is the list the competitor submitted:

**Relevant experience**

*Golden Sunshine Retirement Community*
    *96 elderly units and community building*
    *Three stories*
    *Construction costs: $3,100,000*

*Cameron Place*
    *160 elderly units*
    *Five stories*
    *Construction cost: $3,750,000*

*Guildwood High-rise for the Elderly*
    *95 elderly units*
    *8 stories*
    *Construction cost: $2,530,000*

*Calloway Terrace Community*
    *195 units*
    *Three stories*
    *Construction cost: $3,895,000*

As you can readily see, while the two firms have done different projects, for all intents and purposes, the two lists are identical. On the strength of these two lists, both firms have exactly the same qualifications.

The truth is that most of the firms you compete against are well quali-fied to do the work. You've done great projects. They've done great projects. For every project you can list, they can list another. In the Battle of the Lists the two of you cancel each other out.

Perhaps even more serious is the impact this has on those making the consultant selection decision. Whenever you have to select between two apparently identical options, the only criterion left for making a decision is price! So in this case, who will win the project? The firm with the lower price. In the Battle of the Lists, low price wins every time.

There is another, perhaps greater weakness in the list game. Look at a typical project taken from a real proposal:

| | |
|---|---|
| *Project:* | *Royal Heights Energy Improvements* |
| *Client:* | *Royal Management Corporation* |
| *Const. Cost* | *$285,000* |
| *Description* | *Energy efficient measures including window replacement, pipe wrapping, attic insulation furnace upgrades and caulking were a part of this overall remodeling of 174 Section 8 units and an Administration facility in 36 buildings.* |

This description is totally "neutral." It relates the facts of what was done, but gives no hint as to the value the firm brought to the client and the project. It's a classic, Joe Friday, "Just the facts, ma'am" description.

Where are the lessons learned that will be brought to the next project? Where are the victories and the difficulties overcome? Where are the real challenges that caused you to stop and have work to make that project the success it was?

Equally, if not more, important is how this project shows that you are that "ideal firm" you discovered that the client is seeking. How does this project push the hot buttons you identified?

As written, this description could be of a project on which the consultant completely messed up or, conversely, one on which they saved the client an enormous amount of money. There is no hint given as to what the design firm contributed to the project.

Here's another example of a neutral statement project description. Don't be surprised (or dismayed) if you find that these descriptions are uncomfortably similar to some of your own project listings.

> *River City Sanitary Sewage Collection System and Treatment Plant*
>
> *110,000LF of pressure lines, 10 pump stations and 584 grinder pumps. Provided property plats and descriptions. Prepared 2010 facilities plan update, sewer use ordinance, operation and maintenance manual, user charge program, railroad, TDOT and NPDES permits.*

Not only is this boring, it's really hard to read. Yes, it relates what was done but it tells nothing about the value the consultant brought to the table. And it's a guarantee that your competitor has a similar project.

## So here's what you do

Instead of writing boring, Joe Friday, "Just the facts, ma'am" project descriptions, you are going to use the information and insight you gathered in your research and brainstorming to hard-wire this project experience directly to the client's wish list. Let's go back to the example of brainstorming results we used in discussing cover letters.

The project is a new medical center addition and your answers were these:

**Hot buttons**

- Completing the project within 18 months
- Maintaining positive community relations
- Maintaining ongoing operations during construction
- Control over a very tight budget

**Ideal firm**

- Located within 20 minutes of the project
- Willing to accept input of Board of Directors and doctors
- Full service firm with all in-house disciplines
- Project manager who has extensive medical center experience

**Objections to your firm**

- Located 100 miles away from the project            (true)
- Lacks in-house engineering staff            (true)
- Project manager has little medical center experience            (false)
- Not the firm we've always worked with            (true)

## Competition

Acme Architects      + high quality contract documents
                             − poor reputation for budget control

Ace Architects       + strong project management capability
                             − last project resulted in poor client relations

Long & Short A/E   + worked with client before
                             − high priced

A traditional description of a relevant project might look something like this:

| | |
|---|---|
| *Project:* | *Summit Medical Associates Office* |
| *Client:* | *Summit Medical Associates, LLC* |
| *Const. Cost* | *$1.3 million* |
| *Description* | *Design of new medical office building to house a team of six doctors. Project included 10,000 square feet of office space on two floors with accommodation for a third floor addition in the future.* |

Plenty of firms have done projects like this. From now on you are going to let the client really see the value you bring. This description will focus on the hot button of community relations and the potential objection of your firm being 100 miles from the project site.

| | |
|---|---|
| *Project:* | *Summit Medical Associates Office* |
| *Client:* | *Summit Medical Associates, LLC* |
| *Description* | *This 10,000 square foot medical office was designed for a close-knit team of six doctors with strong ties to their community. In order to ease patient transition to the new location, our design team provided the doctors with a monthly "update newsletter" to be mailed to their patient list. This kept patients informed and excited about the new office. To further reinforce the feeling of community we assigned Jim Travers, who had grown up in the adjacent neighborhood, as project architect.* |

Here's another project description in which tight schedule control and strong communication with the client are featured.

Project:    *New Orthopedic Wing, Children's Hospital*

*When the hospital Board of Directors delayed a crucial decision on funding, the project quickly fell behind schedule by more than six months. To recover the lost time, Smith & Jones initiated a fast-track process in which the end-user doctors and nurses participated in structured design forums. Once the key decisions had been made, we expedited the project by working directly with the hospital and the equipment suppliers to provide equipment to the contractor. The project was completed within the original schedule.*

*"Without the strong and creative leadership exhibited by Smith & Jones, this project would have been at least a year behind schedule."*
*Dr. John Hopkins, Administrator, Children's Hospital*

Descriptions like these give your client real insight into who you are and what you are likely to do for them.

Notice also how the powerful client testimonial has been worked into the project description. Any positive statement from a client can be incorporated with your project stories to add enormous credibility to your statements.

Don't leave the testimonials to languish in fifth generation photocopies of letters at the back of the proposal. They'll never be read! Instead, pull out the really great statements and spread them throughout your proposal. Include them in personal and team profiles, in project approach statements, in your cover letter and in your project descriptions. Testimonials are one of the most powerful persuasion tools you have. Use them!

## Story telling

Remember way back when you were little and your mom was tucking you into bed at night? Do you remember her ever reading you a bedtime list?

Of course you don't. What a ludicrous notion! What child would put up with something so mind-numbing as to be read a list? No, your mother read you stories. She read stories because stories are interesting, they're entertaining, they have fascinating characters who face and overcome challenges. Perhaps most importantly, stories teach lessons. They have morals that allow us to see and understand things that we didn't before.

In short, stories are a whole lot more interesting and valuable as agents of effective communication than are lists. So why do we insist on using lists in our proposals instead of telling stories? Perhaps because we've simply never thought about it.

Let me tell you a story about story-telling.

I was working with a construction company in Washington, D.C. I was helping them write a proposal for a new project in the city. It was a large office building to be built on a very tight, urban site. One of the concerns identified by the client was that their geotechnical testing determined that the site had significant groundwater. During excavation groundwater would fill the hole. The client had wanted to know about the firm's experience with dewatering and how they intended to handle this challenge.

My client's first instinct was to assemble a list of all the jobs on which they had done dewatering. They wanted to demonstrate their considerable expertise in this area by the length of their list.

Let's think about that strategy. Yes, my client had experience in dewatering, but so did all their competitors. Everybody's done this kind of thing and in a list-versus-list shootout, nobody wins.

So I suggested that instead of preparing a list, we were instead going to tell a story. I then asked who was assigned to be the site Superintendent on this project. They answered that it was going to be "Ol' Pete." It turned out that Pete was one of those crusty old construction superintendents who's been doing this work for 100 years and knows his way around a construction site.

I said, "Let's get Pete on the phone." So we call him on his cell phone—he's out on a construction site somewhere—and I asked, "Pete, what was the toughest, worst ground water problem you have ever run into on a construction project?" Pete replied, "That's an easy question. I'll never forget that one. We were building an underground parking garage. We got down about 20 feet and hit this underground river."

Now think about the images that are coming into your mind as you ponder the concept of "hitting an underground river." They've got to be pretty formidable—from great gushers coming out of the ground; construction equipment and small children being swept away in the torrent; women screaming and grown men running for cover! It's an exciting and engaging image.

I said, "Pete, wow! What did you do?" And like the good construction superintendent he is, he said, "It was no big deal. We dug a moat around the site and diverted it while we built the garage."

Now the images have expanded to medieval castles, Herculean feats, and the power of man to tame mighty rivers. This is some pretty cool stuff! Not something you find in your everyday proposal.

Remember, our choice was between giving them a list of "projects on which we've done dewatering" or telling the story of Pete Versus the Underground River. Which would you prefer to read? Which sounds like it would be more interesting and memorable? Of course we passed on the list and told the story of Pete Versus the Underground River.

Telling the story accomplished a couple of very important things. First, it assured that the client would actually read it. Who, browsing through a proposal and coming across something as unexpected as that, would not? Second, it achieved something called the "Sinatra Effect." This is a concept noted by Chip and Dan Heath in their highly recommended book, *Made to Stick*.

If you remember the old Frank Sinatra song, *New York, New York*, you'll know the line that says, "If I can make it there, I'll make it anywhere." I don't need to tell you that I've made it in Topeka and Sioux Falls and Albuquerque. I just need to tell you that I made it in New York. Okay, that's good enough!

Telling the story of Pete Versus the Underground River achieves the same Sinatra Effect. Essentially, if Pete can handle that situation, he can certainly handle anything that our project is going to throw at him. And that's all we needed to accomplish. We didn't include any list of other projects. And we made it to the short list.

## Personal profiles

You used to call them résumés. But don't do that anymore.

A résumé is the document you use when you're looking for a new employer. A personal profile is what you use when you're trying to persuade a client to retain your firm for a new project. The difference is in the detail and the emphasis that's given to the information.

Here is an example of an actual "résumé," pulled from a proposal and typical of the sort you see in countless design firm proposals (the name and identifying details have been changed).

*Mr. John Doe, P.E., A.I.C.P.*
*Manager of Municipal Engineering*

*Areas of Expertise*
*Traffic Engineering, transportation planning, storm water analysis, priority watershed planning, project management, capital improvement programming, utility system planning.*

*Education*
*M.S., Urban and Regional Planning, University of South Carolina, 1978*
*B.S., Civil Engineering, Clemson University, 1974*

*Registration*
*Professional Engineer in Iowa (#345-1489) Illinois (#7890537590), Wisconsin (#38274585679) and Kansas (#2849573)*

*Professional Affiliations*
*American Council of Engineering Companies*
*American Public Works Association*
*American Planning Association*
*American Institute of Certified Planners*
*Institute of Transportation Engineers*

*Employment*
*Smith & Jones Engineering*
*City of Des Moines, IA*
*City of Madison, WI*

*Experience*
*Has extensive experience directed to municipalities for traffic engineering, utility design, comprehensive plan development, zoning and*

subdivision ordinances, transportation, buildings and recreational facilities. Has considerable experience in short- and long-range planning for communities of several thousand to one million people.

Prepared and completed long-range studies of water supply, sewer, and collection systems and developed storm water management plans. Storm water analysis included detention and sedimentation basins to reduce sediment flows. Has been project manager of numerous priority watershed studies and designs in the Midwest. Has provided project management and quality assurance for transportation projects including design for residential streets, major arterials, and industrial parks and studies related to traffic and corridors, needs, safety, and location. Also served as city engineer for several communities and townships in the southern portion of the state.

Related Projects

Sioux Highway
Project manager for reconstruction of a half-mile section of road that included a water main, sewer interceptor and storm sewer.

Matthews Road
Project manager on a half-mile reconstruction of an arterial roadway under joint jurisdiction of two communities. Project involved a new water main, storm sewer and roadway.

Broadway Corridor Traffic Study
The City and the Community Development Authority developed a plan to redevelop the Turner Street Corridor from 51st Street to Highway 27. As a part of the development team, Smith & Jones was contracted to undertake a traffic study of the Turner Street Corridor to determine the impact of the proposed development. As a part of this work, made traffic projections of the new development, assessed impact on the current road network and recommended future improvements to the system.

Broad River/Shining Creek Watershed
This project involved six separate studies in three different communities in the metropolitan area. The watersheds studied ranged in area from 12 to 800 acres. As a result of the studies, eight separate Best Management Practices were approved for design and construction.

Did you actually read the whole thing? My guess is that, at best, you scanned it. More likely, you started into it, read a little, got bored quickly, and then jumped straight down to here where the text (hopefully) gets interesting again!

That's exactly what your clients do. Reading the colorless details of someone else's career is among life's more tedious tasks. And we avoid it whenever possible.

Since the point of the proposal is to *persuade* the client to choose you, why not rebuild your profile to make it an exciting, vital and fascinating part of the persuasion process?

To start, let's analyze the profile above.

First, it's written in the mode of the traditional résumé, which is an attempt to find employment. It relates the full breadth of Mr. Doe's education, affiliation and experience. These might be of interest to a prospective employer but would hold little appeal to a client with a specific project in mind.

Second, it is entirely possible to imagine a context in which a client would value Mr. Doe for both his *extensive experience in buildings and recreational facilities* and his ability to conduct *long-range studies of water supply, sewer and collection systems and develop storm water management plans*. But most clients are thinking of a much more specific project application that would demand one or the other, but not both.

When our friend Mr. Doe lists everything he can do, it makes the résumé longer, reduces the chance that the client will read the whole thing and actually dilutes the impact of the skills he has that are relevant to the project at hand.

Fortunately, we can fine tune and focus Mr. Doe's profile using the research and brainstorming that you will have already conducted. Let's go through that exercise.

The project is a watershed study and came up with the following brainstorming answers:

**Hot buttons**

- Long term recommendations for commercial development
- Contribution to existing GIS database
- Working closely with county engineering staff

## Ideal firm

- Extensive stormwater design experience
- Familiarity with local politics of development
- Success in community relations with small towns

Here's how Mr. Doe might assemble a personal profile targeted directly to this client.

*Your Project Engineer*

*Mr. John Doe, P.E., A.I.C.P., will be the project engineer for your watershed study. With more than twenty years of lessons learned from small municipalities like yours throughout the upper Midwest, John is a recognized leader in finding common ground between local commercial interests, long-range community planning and the needs of the natural environment.*

- *For the town of Podunk, a community similar in size to yours, John worked closely with the engineering staff to combine the data from the 400-acre watershed study with the town's ongoing effort to build a GIS database. The town engineer estimated the effort saved close to $10,000 in data collection costs.*

- *The Broad River/Shining Creek Watershed project involved six separate studies in three different communities. With strong pressure for commercial development, and with each community working to attract business, John was required to balance the sometimes conflicting interests of local governmental officials, staff and commercial developers. His long-term design recommendations were praised by all concerned and eight separate Best Management Practices were approved for design and construction.*

*"John's ability to work productively with small towns was most appreciated. He kept us all working together."*

*James P. Gilmore, Mayor, Town of Podunk*

- *Since joining Smith & Jones Engineering 15 years ago, John has conducted 36 stormwater studies and designs, more than any other engineer in the region. His recommendations have been valued by government officials, staff and developers and he has even been a speaker at the national conference of the American Planning Association.*

*Reference*

*Ms. Janice Woodcock*
*Planner, Town of Clearville*
*(123) 456-7890*

*Ms. Woodcock worked closely with John during the watershed study and can give insight into his ability to work with town engineering staff.*

*John was selected for this assignment from among our talented engineering staff because he, more than anyone else, combines the stormwater planning expertise with a keen understanding of the dynamics of development in smaller communities.*

*John is currently working on a similar study for Cooper County and will be available to begin work on your project on September 1.*

Notice how this profile didn't mention anything about his experience in traffic studies or the design of recreational buildings. The content of this profile focused exclusively on those things that are up front in the client's mind. Should another project come up that concerns traffic engineering, John's profile will say little or nothing about watershed studies.

You'll also notice how this profile is considerably shorter and far easier and more pleasant to read. It actually tells stories that are intriguing. The bottom line: this is a person that the client wants on their project team.

## Colin Powell's résumé

I want you to think about Colin Powell's résumé. What might it look like? Essentially he has two choices. The first choice runs 20 or more pages and begins when he was 15 and cutting the grass for Mrs. Gilhooley next door and covers everything he did over his career until it concludes with his being Secretary of State. It would be incredibly long, incredibly boring and no one would ever get to the punchline at the end. They'd stop reading long before the good part.

The second option has only two entries. One says, "Chairman of the Joint Chiefs of Staff." The second says, "Secretary of State of the United States of America."

Any questions?

Once more, this is the Sinatra Effect at work. If you see those two entries, you can reasonably fill in the rest for yourself. You can easily imagine that he's done some other, pretty impressive things that don't need to be detailed. You can easily conclude that if he can do those two things he can do all the rest, too.

Think back to Pete versus the Underground River. You accomplished this same effect by telling that story. Every single project on which you've ever worked has these hero stories. You were presented with an incredible obstacle and you overcame it. If you can accomplish that on someone else's project, we can certainly handle what the client's project has to offer. Collect these stories. Hang on to them. Document them. Then re-tell them.

# Testimonials

If you've been following along, you've noticed how I have used testimonials throughout the various sections of the proposal. As I've said before, testimonials are among the most powerful marketing and sales tools you can use. Put another way, your clients are much better at marketing you that you are. So use testimonials as often as you can.

A testimonial is an existing client, with nothing to gain by it, volunteering to endorse your services. They are recommending that one of their peers—your current, prospective client—purchase your services.

Every firm has letters of recommendation. They are often photocopied and included at the end of your proposal. The problem is, in that location, they are never read. A client, with insufficient time to read your proposal, scans through the document and finds a page which is obviously a photocopy of an old letter that recommends your services. They mentally note that you have clients who are willing to recommend you (who doesn't?) and they continue to turn pages without ever actually reading the letter. Your job is to extract the valuable statements from the letter and make them easily accessible to the reader.

On the next page is an actual testimonial letter from a client (a department of the Federal government). Again, names have been changed.

*John Q. Semour Construction Co.*
*Federal Treasury Building Field Office*
*123 4th Street, NE*
*Washington, DC 20000*

*Attn:   Ms. Mary Green*
*Construction Executive*

*Re:     U.S. Treasury Building*

*We refer to our Construction Management Agreement with you dated September 18, 1999, Article 9.8, Substantial Completion, and to the fully executed Certificate of Substantial Completion for Level 5 (six pages dated June 3, 2002, copy attached). We forward a copy of this certificate to you with great pleasure. We congratulate you and your staff, both in the field and in the main office, for achieving this first substantial completion milestone at Level 5.*

*Semour's on-time delivery of the completed fifth floor, at a level of cleanliness, fit and finish seldom seen in our industry, is an achievement for which you should all be proud. Please extend our congratulations and thanks to all of your staff involved.*

*As a result of your achievement, we are pleased to look forward to your equally successful and on-time completion of the remaining areas of the building. Please do not hesitate to ask if there is anything we can do to assist you in achieving your goals. All of us here at NewTown Properties maintain genuine enthusiasm working with you to successfully complete all areas.*

*Again, congratulations to all of you.*

*Sincerely,*

*Michael Jones*

If you managed to wade through the first paragraph and hadn't fallen asleep, you would discover a real marketing jewel in the second paragraph. But there is little likelihood that a client would get that far. You will also notice that the letter is dated 2002. As long as the date was attached, the letter was obsolete by 2007.

Instead of simply photocopying the letter and inserting it in your proposal, pull out the really good stuff and use it where it has the most impact. When you do this, you discover that this letter contains at least five separate testimonials, none of which are tied to an obsolete date.

**Hot button** is schedule:

> *"We congratulate you and your staff, both in the field and in the main office, for achieving this first substantial completion milestone."*

**Hot button** is quality work:

> *"Semour's on-time delivery of the completed fifth floor, at a level of cleanliness, fit and finish seldom seen in our industry, is an achievement for which you should all be proud."*

**Hot button** is client relations:

> *"Please extend our congratulations and thanks to all of your staff involved."*

> *"All of us here at NewTown Properties maintain genuine enthusiasm working with you."*

**Hot button** is long-term relationship

> *"As a result of your achievement, we are pleased to look forward to your equally successful and on-time completion of the remaining areas of the building."*

These testimonials can be used anywhere in the proposal where you want to make a powerful impact and reinforce a point you have discovered in your research and brainstorming.

# 10
# Let's Really Go Off the Deep End

Let's take a minute and go back to that proposal-writing workshop I conducted (described in Chapter 6) and remind ourselves about that 18-second clock that gets you into the short-list pile or the rejects. If that's true (and I've never spoken to anyone who's participated on a selection panel who denies it), then our challenge becomes one of communicating the essence of your proposal in the shortest possible time.

Fortunately there are some masters of communication from whom we can learn. It's an odd source, but there are a lot of lessons to be learned. In my ongoing study of the best ways to get a point across quickly, I haven't yet found anyone who's better at it than magazine designers and editors.

The method in which magazines are usually sold faces many of the same challenges that you do when you're trying to sell your design or construction services. They too have about 18 seconds in which to convince you to buy the magazine.

How so? Consider this: You're standing in the checkout line of the grocery store. While you're waiting for your turn you are scanning the maga- zine covers on the rack beside you. Their version of making the short list is to have the magazine end up in your shopping cart.

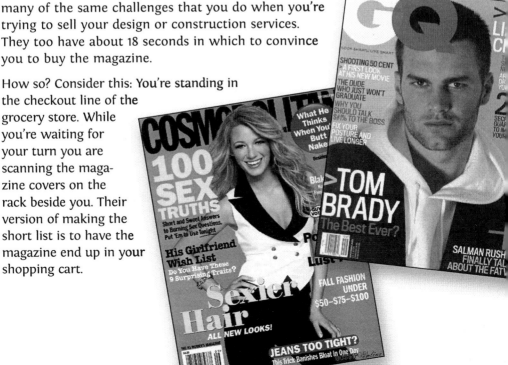

So the first thing they do is to take their entire table of contents and put it right there on the front cover. Not only do they put it on the front cover, they do it in a manner that is provocative and intriguing and curiosity-provoking. Take a look at these magazine covers—there it is right there: "The sex position they lust for!" Bingo! What's that about? I want to know. Or "Look Like a Champ." Hey, I want to look like an NFL quarterback, so I pick it up and start looking. Those short headlines are known in the business as "teasers" for obvious reasons. They want to tease you a little, make you curious enough to pick up the magazine.

By taking their content and putting it on the cover, the magazines have persuaded you to take the first step, which is to pick the magazine up off the shelf. Once you've picked it up you start reviewing it in exactly the same manner that we described earlier about the first glance through a proposal. You start flipping with your thumb from the back. And your eye is scanning this document asking, "Is there something in here that is of interest to me?" The same 18-second clock is ticking away.

The interesting thing about magazines and the way they communicate, and this has been very carefully structured, is that every article has been written to be read on at least five levels. As I'm flipping through the magazine, my eye is skimming and scanning and looking for something that might be of interest. Let's say I flip to here:

The first thing my eye sees is a big, bold headline, in big, bold letters. It's so easy to read that you can't not read it. The editors consciously write them with short, easy-to-read words. As soon as your eye hits those five words, you've already read them. And now you've read the article one time because the headline is, in fact, the article condensed into five words.

You now make a snap judgment that only takes a split second. You ask yourself, "Is this something of interest to me?" If it's not, you keep flipping. If it is, you read the article a second time. But you don't start reading the body of the text, instead you read the sub-heading. And in that subtitle the editor has conveniently given you the article a second time in another format. It's a little longer and more detailed, but still short and easy to read. Maybe it takes three seconds to read but you're willing to invest that time and you've now read the article twice. You now make a second evaluation.

Is this still of interest to me? If "No," you keep flipping pages. But if it is still of interest, you read the article a third time. (You're still standing in the checkout line, remember.) But you still don't read the text of the actual article itself, because they've given you pictures. And every picture has a caption. The pictures are interesting and the captions are very easy and fast to read.

They've also given you "mini-articles" in the form of sidebars that address related topics. They've also used what are called "pull quotes," those short sentence fragments that are pulled from the body of the article and put into a large, bold font in a box or in the middle of the page. The editors select these carefully because they are provocative and intriguing. They're another example of those teasers because they entice you to want to read the rest of the article.

Now you've read the article four separate times, but even four times didn't take very long. Just the time you had standing in the checkout line. And having read the article four times and wanting to read it again, this time in detail, you're ready to commit and you throw it into your shopping cart and buy the magazine.

At that point, the magazine editor and graphic designer have done their jobs. They sold the magazine. In your case, once you've made the short list, the proposal has done its job.

Something interesting happens once you get the magazine home. You may or may not ever actually get around to reading that article and the publisher doesn't care. You paid for it and that's all they wanted. Just like you don't much care whether or not your client actually reads your entire proposal. The magazine made it into your shopping cart and your proposal made it to the short list.

# The alternative

Now imagine flipping through the same magazine, only this time there is nothing on the cover except the name of the magazine and some generic, uninteresting picture. The table of contents lists uninspiring headings for articles which, when you turn to them, have only text, a few tiny, unidentified pictures, a series of lists and no "back story" of any sort. How long do you suppose you'd browse? Would you even last 18 seconds?

That's what goes through your client's mind when she flips through your proposal and sees nothing but wall-to-wall text, lists and trite statements. Your 18-second clock is ticking and nothing is jumping out at her. She sees your pages but the content of those pages is not transferring itself to her brain. There is a physical effort involved in reading the material you provide. She just isn't up to that effort and doesn't have that kind of time.

So let's learn from these master communicators—the magazines—who have found a way to put forward key pieces of information very, very quickly, in ways that pique the readers' interest and persuade them to buy the magazine.

Your first instinct might be that these techniques are far too unprofessional to ever be used by a professional design firm. But this isn't about professionalism or lack of it. This is about finding ways to get your clients to see and to understand what it is that you're putting in front of them. There are many firms beginning to use these kinds of quick communication techniques to very good effect.

## WK Dickson

One firm that has been experimenting with a variety of these techniques is WK Dickson, a multi-disciplined consulting firm specializing in community infrastructure, including transportation planning and design, environmental and water resources engineering, urban planning and development, structural engineering and geospatial technology. I think it's important to know these areas in which the firm is active because they aren't disciplines in which you would at first think clients are receptive to non-traditional approaches. But clients, regardless of their company, agency or discipline are also human beings and they get tired of being bored to death.

As David Ogilvy, the father of modern advertising, once said, "You can't bore your customer into buying your product." It's the same with your proposal. You can't bore your client into selecting you.

Look at these examples of actual proposals that have been used successfully to win real projects. The secrets to their success is that they:

1. Stand out from all the others in the pile and attract the client's attention;
2. Get their message across quickly;
3. Make it easy to find and access the information they contain.

Imagine that you're a member of the selection panel and one of your personal hot buttons is highway and creek crossings. Where do you suppose you're going to go? You're going to turn immediately to page 12. And you may or may not bother with any of the other topics. What if it's environmental permitting that interests you the most? You'll want to find out immediately what the firm has to say about that. Of course, the topics that are shown on the cover weren't chosen randomly. They were put there because a brainstorming session identified them as critical decision factors.

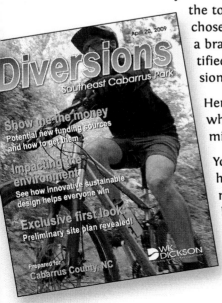

Here's another proposal which the firm has submitted for a win.

You can clearly see how many of the techniques used here have been derived directly from the magazine model of fast communication. The cover is attractive and offers a quick summary, in teaser fashion, of the key contents. Articles have a nice big headline, the page is attractively designed, there are wonderful pictures (not always of projects) with captions and there are pull quotes and sidebars. The reader is not forced to read the body of the text in order to extract the information from the proposal.

One of the things that I want to make very clear is that when you use techniques of this kind, do not do so because it is cute or gimmicky. You should use these techniques because your objective is to communicate ideas and information quickly and effectively to clients. These are simply excellent communication techniques for achieving those goals.

Will this kind of magazine cover approach be an appropriate response for every situation? Absolutely not. There are countless different ways to creatively set your proposal apart from the competition, address the client's concerns and present your firm in an attractive and interesting manner.

Here is another proposal that took a completely different approach. Efird Sutphin Pearce is a small architectural practice in Greensboro, N.C. They responded to an RFP from North Carolina State University. The project was to renovate and replace an existing food

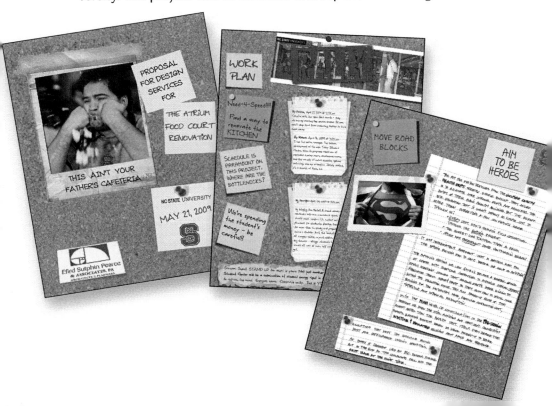

court in the center of campus that had originally been built in the early 1970s. It was an extremely high-profile project and ESP, who previously had only done a few small projects for N. C. State, felt they had little or no chance to make even the short list. But they wanted to do something very different and put themselves on the University's radar screen.

I worked with ESP on this proposal. First, we started brainstorming and came up with a very strange idea. Since the existing facility had been built so long ago, we decided to base the proposal on the theme, "This Ain't Your Father's Cafeteria." That was the hot button that we wanted to push. The existing facility was already more than one generation old, so we decided to make a reference back by a full generation by using the *Animal House* movie images and letting the client know that we understand that "this is not going to be what facilities like this used to be." We decided to use the visual theme of the cork board with push pins and post-it notes to evoke the idea of a vibrant, active student center on a college campus.

As you might imagine, it was hard for a review committee member to not pick up this proposal. Overwhelming curiosity would drive anyone to open this to see what the heck we were thinking—or smoking!—which is exactly what we wanted to have happen!

This next page explained the firm's Approach to the Project. It was summarized in a single page that replicated a bulletin board. The hot button on this job was that the money to pay for the project was coming out of student fees, which wasn't a terribly popular idea around campus. The university was trying to build support for the project. They had already launched a web site on which students were encouraged to give feedback via a chat room and we captured some of the comments that had already been made. This page appeared just like this in the proposal.

This next page tells a hero story. It was our equivalent of Pete Versus the Underground River, and it addressed the hot button issue that the facility would have to stay open at all times during the renovation. It tells the story of another project on which ESP proposed some very innovative methods that allowed the facility to stay open and saved the client money at the same time.

The way it was presented here made it not only easy but actually kind of fun to read. The review panel had never seen anything quite like that before. It invited them to read it. Imagine doing your "left-thumb-quick-flip-through" and coming across this page. You'd stop and take a second look for sure.

In this process, using these non-traditional techniques, we managed to get the client's attention. They reacted to something that was different and interesting. Not only had they never seen anything like it before, but because the ESP proposal was easy to access and read, the University realized that the firm had some really good ideas and suggestions. They could easily read those ideas and see very quickly that the firm would bring value to the project.

Forty-nine firms submitted proposals on this project. And remember, my client, who had had very little experience with N. C. State, assumed that they didn't stand a chance. This proposal helped them make it to the short list of three firms. You'll find out what happened next in the following chapter!

# 11

# PowerPoint Is *Not* Your Presentation

Way back in Chapter 2 we talked about the three-stage process clients use to select a design firm. At each stage they are looking for answers to different sets of questions.

In this third and final stage—the presentation or interview—the questions they want answered include:

- What can I expect from you on this project?
- Can you stand in front of a group of people and be understood?
- How do you handle it when someone throws you a curve ball?
- Do you get flustered?
- Are you smooth?
- Do you answer honestly?
- What's it actually like to be in the same room with you?
- Since we're going to be spending the next six months up close and personal together working on this project, can I stand being with you?
- Are you the kind of person that I'd actually like to work with?

These questions can only be answered when you're there in the room, in person, responding on the spot.

## And now you've made the short list

Your client has carefully reviewed all the qualifications (education, experience, approach) and has satisfied herself that each of the five firms has the technical capability of doing this job. The project will be designed and built and it will work.

How does she sort through these remaining five?

Let's take a moment and drift back to Chapter 3, where we discussed the notion of selling "intangibles." If you recall, we said that a client, when looking to purchase professional design services, doesn't have the advantage of "test driving" your firm before you do the work. They have to take a leap of faith that your firm is the right one and that they've made a good decision. That's why they go through this rigorous process and ask these multiple questions in different formats and venues. Because, at the end of the day, the only thing your client has got to go on is that moment when you look them in the eye and shake their hands and say, "I'm going to look after you." and they say, "You know what? we believe you. We trust you. We've got confidence in you."

That's why, when you get to the presentation stage, the client needs to be able to look you in the eye and ask a tough question. The prospective client can tell a great deal about you by the way you answer. It's trust and a sense of confidence that clients are looking for and you need to be able to provide that in your interview.

So the objective in an interview or presentation is to provide an opportunity for personal, face-to-face communication that allows the client to establish confidence in the decision they are about to make.

In stark contrast, have you ever served on a review panel or selection committee? This isn't a privilege, it's a sentence! All the presentations run together, they all look and sound the same, and by the time it's over you can't remember or distinguish one from another. You're fast asleep, if not brain dead.

How does a design firm typically go about developing a presentation? Here's where they—you—always start.

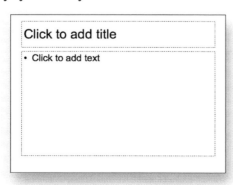

In fact, more often than not, you don't even start here. You pull up the last winning presentation that you did, do a "Save As," and then start changing dates and names. Isn't PowerPoint great!?

But you don't want your client getting bored from just reading your bullet points. With PowerPoint, you can put in pictures or clever diagrams. PowerPoint then goes even further and asks which background you'd like to use? Then it provides dozens of ready-made backgrounds and color schemes.

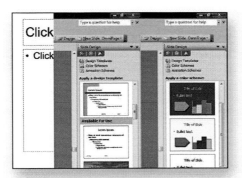

And if you're not satisfied with the options that the software provides, there is an entire culture built around making PowerPoint even easier for you. Go online and Google "PowerPoint Backgrounds" and you will discover thousands of them waiting for you. Here's one that I found, for example. It's hip, fresh, cool and free. It offers a "cool blue tech background for PowerPoint. The edges look like copper wires or circuit boards. It would be great for a presentation involving technology."

With all due respect to the people who have worked hard to create your supporting material, how dumb do you think your clients would have to be to decide that they will hire the team that had the blue color scheme instead of the green one? Or to think that "you had that attractive background so we'll hire you"? Is there somewhere on the face of this planet, a client who is so stupid as to say, "Oh, let's hire them. They had a background with lines that sort of looked like circuit boards. They must be technically competent!"

Your clients are very smart, savvy, sophisticated people.

The problem with PowerPoint is that it has been designed as a tool that is convenient for the presenter. It has not been designed as a tool that is convenient for the audience. And it truly does make a presenter's life easy. This is a great tool for organizing your thoughts: Click here to add title. Click here to add text. Let's add a diagram. And snap! you've got a presentation. Then, to make things even more convenient, you've got all your cheat notes right up there on the screen so you don't have to remember anything. You can simply stand there and read to your audience!

But . . . think again about your objectives in a presentation and about this multi-stage process. If, in fact, you could accomplish those objectives by simply reading your client a document, why don't you just send them an email that they can read for themselves?

Because that's not what you're trying to accomplish.

## The good news about PowerPoint

Having said all those nasty things, I want you to know that I use PowerPoint for the vast majority of my presentations—and I make a lot of them!—but I just never use it the way they designed it to be used. More about that later.

No question: PowerPoint is a powerful presentation tool. But it is not the *only* presentation tool. You'll see in this chapter that there are many different presentation approaches. Every single one of them begins by asking, "Who are we presenting to?" "What do I know about this client?" "What are they looking for and what's the best way to communicate to them?" Remember, the objective of the presentation is to get inside their heads and stay there. At the end of the day you want your client to say, "I want that! That's exactly what I want. I'm excited about that firm."

Unfortunately you can't achieve that objective with this:

There is a psychological concept known as "cognitive overload." In essence, it says that the human brain is like one of those plastic 2-liter Coke bottles. It will actually hold quite a bit, but the opening is rather small and you can only get so much in at a time. Imagine taking an empty one of those bottles and trying to pour a pail of water into it. How much of the water do you suppose would actually end up in the bottle? And how much would be splashed all over the ground?

When you communicate, you're trying to pour your knowledge into your customers' brains so that they say, "Oh, wow! I understand it. I want that!" But when you use communication techniques that induce cognitive overload, most of the content of what you're saying simply spills out all over the ground.

In developing an effective presentation, your goal should be to provide information in a way that maximizes your audience's ability to process and remember it. But it turns out that one of the least effective ways to accomplish this, the way that induces cognitive overload most quickly, is to have information come to you in both written and spoken form at the same time. Which is exactly what PowerPoint, used in the intended manner, does. When you have a screen full of bullet points which the presenter is reading aloud while the audience simultaneously reads them silently, nothing sticks.

If what you tend to throw up on the screen is working at odds with your objectives, the dynamics and physical organization of most presentations make it even worse. Remember that your objective is to make a personal connection, to communicate well enough that you connect on a personal, even an emotional, level.

What are the dynamics of a typical PowerPoint presentation? First, everyone is sitting, facing the screen. Second, the presenter is either standing off in a dark corner or standing in front of the audience but with his back to them, and everyone is reading together, the presenter out loud and the audience silently. And all the valuable content of the presentation is spilling all over the ground.

I recently attended a half-day program discussing the healthcare industry in this country. It was held in a hotel ballroom with perhaps 200 people in the audience. There were some very well educated, sophisticated and knowledgeable experts on the panel and as speakers. There was a giant screen at the front of the room and way off to the side, in the corner, in the dark, was a podium where each speaker would stand to present. One of the speakers was a doctor who was obviously very intelligent, but she was about 5'3" at best. The podium came up to her chest, there was a microphone in front of her face and she was in the dark. Her presentation consisted of dozens of PowerPoint slides filled with bullet points that she read out loud while we read silently, and I don't remember a word she said or even what she was talking about. Which is really too bad because she was an intelligent person who probably had some important things to say. Yet none of it sunk in with any of the audience because of the way it was set up.

**Fundamental point:** Whatever is up on the wall in your slides or your boards or whatever props you might have is not your presentation. *You are the presentation.*

Let's repeat that: *You are the presentation.* Whatever you have up on the wall is not the presentation. It is simply there to reinforce, augment, decorate and supplement the message that you, personally, as a human being are bringing to that audience so that you can connect with them.

If you can rely on the words on the wall to convey the message, then save everyone the hassle and just send a memo. If that would successfully communicate your message, then a presentation is an inappropriate medium to use.

But if a memo won't suffice, let's make sure you design and deliver a presentation that accomplishes the goals you want.

## So what should be on the wall?

If whatever is up on the wall in your slides or your boards or whatever props you might have is not your presentation, then what should be up on the wall? What is the purpose of having visual materials?

The visual materials that you provide are there only to enhance, support and reinforce the points that *you*, the real essence of the presentation, make. Take a look at this photo and decide for yourself what the real message of this presentation is.

**Presenters at a conference**

Do you see how, regardless of what is projected on the wall, the human beings are always the presentation? And in this case, the message that the human beings are sending so powerfully overrides the message in the visuals as to make the image hilarious. So once again, the visuals are not your presentation. You are the presentation.

But let's talk for a moment about how you can develop supporting visuals that reinforce your message without inducing cognitive overload. While this isn't the place for a course in slide and visual presentation design, I encourage you to investigate some of the better practitioners of this art, including Garr Reynolds through his book, *Presentation Zen*, and Nancy Duarte, through her book, *Slide:ology*.

Let's look at some common PowerPoint slide examples and see how they can be improved. In each case the "before" image is an actual slide taken from a presentation made by a design or construction firm. Any identifying information has been removed.

## Slide #1

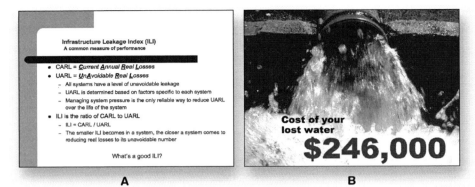

Slide A tries to educate the client on the engineering practice needed to calculate the amount of water that leaks from a municipal water supply system. It ends up being more like a 4000-level college course, complete with a test at the end! Is all of this information necessary? When you ask yourselves the important question, "What is my point and why should the client care?," you will discover that *none* of this matters. It could all be much better summarized and reinforced by a slide that looked more like Slide B.

This focuses on the magnitude of the problem at hand. Instead of becoming distracted by the minute detail of the calculations, it focuses on the problem, and then the presenter (that's you!) can be the solution.

## Slide #2

It's not uncommon for the client to want to review the key members of your team during your presentation. And it's appropriate to include a slide that highlights an individual.

But Slide A contains far too much information and will result in cognitive overload. Even if it doesn't, it will certainly distract the audience who will be reading on their own while you try to speak. Instead, try to determine the most important point you want to make about the individual and keep the visual simple.

The audience will spend next to no time reading Slide B, then return their attention to the human presenter to learn more about the person who will be working on their project.

**Slide #3**

A　　　　　　　　　　　　　　　　　　　B

Slide A contains a table full of data. Not only will it be difficult to read on the screen, data tables like this are hard to interpret without spending a great deal of time in analysis.

What is the point of the data? What is the point you are trying to make with the data? Instead of asking the audience to study the table and find the lesson they're supposed to learn from it, your visual should do that for them. And if you can do that in a visual way—here using colored graphs instead of numerical charts—you'll make your point much more quickly and clearly.

## Slide #4

Here is a classic example of "Click Here to Add Title" that has turned into
a bad case of cognitive overload.

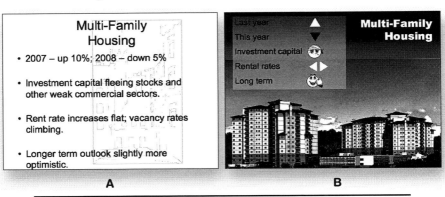

Not only is it difficult to read and interpret the information, the creator
of the slide decided that the text alone is boring and needed some visual
interest. The clip art image behind the text only serves to make it even
more difficult to read. Your visuals should always interpret the data for
your audience. Let them see the "punch line" right away, then they can
switch back to listening to you as you discuss the implications of the
information.

## Slide #5

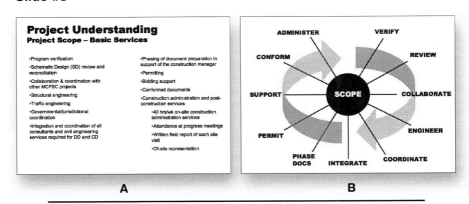

Sometimes it's necessary to have a list of items on your slide. But a standard PowerPoint bullet point list is never the way to present it. This
slide, which lists the sequence of tasks to be completed in a scope of

work, results in classic cognitive overload and will have everyone reading the small print and paying no attention to you.

Instead, let your list have some dynamic flair to it. In this case, the list is presented in a way that implies the sequence of activities on the project and can be easily scanned. Then the focus and the conversation goes back to the presenter.

The rule for visuals is this: *Visuals should be made up of visual elements.* Words are not visual, they are textual. So keep the words off your slides and instead keep the visual focus on pictures and diagrams.

If you look at the following collection of visuals, you can instantly get a sense of what each image is conveying to you without using a single word. The arrows pointing to the circle in the center talk about collaboration and cooperation. The diagram implies teamwork and coming together. The image speaks far more loudly than any words.

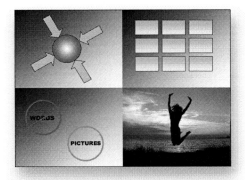

Likewise, without a single word, the matrix of rectangles tells a story about a set of elements making up a whole. And the photo of the woman leaping up speaks loudly about energy, exuberance, excitement and enthusiasm. It tells that story instantly, allowing the audience to listen to you. Remember that *you* are the presentation: engage them in a conversation about how your team will bring that excitement, energy and enthusiasm to their project.

# 12

# Audience Attention Levels

Let's talk for a minute about the dynamics of your audience.

Think back to the last presentation you attended. Maybe it lasted an hour. Did you maintain absolute, unflinching, concentrated focus through the entire presentation? Of course you didn't. Your mind drifts. It wanders off to other thoughts—things going on at work, things you have to remember to take care of at home, an errand you have to run that evening. Regardless, your mind wanders all over. The human mind is an enormously difficult thing to control.

As your presentation proceeds, the audience's level of attention also varies. The good news is that it changes in ways that are highly predictable. At the beginning of anyone's presentation or speech, the audience is paying a high level of attention. They are thinking, "This is new. I haven't heard this person speak before. Is there something I'm going to learn? What's of value to me?" Early on they are going to be paying close attention.

However, once the speaker gets into the details of the presentation, the audience's attention level falls off. Quite steeply actually. As the presentation rolls on, the audience members are off to many different places—everywhere except here listening to the speaker! Then, as they sense it's coming to an end—"It was a 30 minute presentation, it's been 25 minutes, I guess they'll be wrapping up soon"—they start paying attention because they know they can pick up the gist in the summary. And the speaker always oblige by giving a summary.

Good speech writers know how this dynamic works and they will insert what we call "attention spikes" Into o their presentations. They will put a joke in the speech, which brings everyone back. Or they will tell an interesting anecdote that will bring the audience back to the speaker. But it will only be temporary, since we know they'll drift off again.

Now imagine that same presentation being given twice. Once at 9:00 in the morning and again at 3:00 in the afternoon. Imagine the difference in the state of the audience's minds at those two times! At 9:00 they are fresh and clear, they've just had a good sleep and probably their morning coffee, and they are ready to pay attention. At 3:00 in the afternoon, their blood sugar is falling, their brains are looking forward to the end of the day, they are still digesting lunch, and a short nap sounds like the best thing going.

When you design a presentation you must take into account the time of day that it's going to be delivered because the dynamics of the audience changes dramatically.

## The typical approach

Now that you know the dynamics of audience attention level work this way, how is the typical presentation designed?

The presenting team walks in when the audience's attention level is very high and they use this time to say things such as:

> "Good morning. We're really pleased to have this opportunity to present to you today. We'd like to take a moment to tell you a little bit more about our firm and allow you to get to know us personally. Before we get started we'd like to tell you about the history of our firm. We've been in business since 1932. Our firm was founded by James Founder and we've since grown steadily. We now have 10 offices in three states. . . ."

As the team goes on, imagine that you're watching the dial on an Attention-O-Meter attached to the audience. It's falling fast! They are drifting off. And they're drifting off just as the team is about to head into the meat of its presentation, where they'll explain why they should be the obvious choice. But the audience has left the room. They're gone and not listening to all the great reasons why they should hire the firm. They miss the punch line.

Then, when the audience does come back for the close, what do we typically do? We wrap up by saying,

> "I'd like to thank you again for allowing us to be here today and reinforce just how important this project is to us and tell you how committed we are to your satisfaction."

So the presentation opened with trite statements. It also closed with trite statements and all the good stuff was put into the part where the audience was missing. It is any wonder that people on selection panels have a great challenge to separate one firm from another. They saw five firms and when they go off to deliberate they can't remember anyone standing out: "Was that the guy in the purple shirt or the one in the green shirt? I don't remember."

## A surprising secret door to your client's mind

You've always known that going either first or last in the order of presentations offers an advantage. The reason is that the firms that presents first and last are more likely to stand out in the minds of the client review team members. Did you also know that the same rule applies within the span of your own presentation?

To be successful in front of a jury, a good trial lawyer must be effective as both a presenter and a persuader. After all, the lawyer is trying to sell something to the jury: the idea that a defendant is either guilty or innocent. Trial lawyers have always known that, in order to persuade a jury, they can rely on two principles: the doctrines of *primacy* and *recency*.

The doctrine of primacy says that you should always lead off with your strongest statement. This catches your audience off-guard and leaves a dramatic and indelible first impression.

The doctrine of recency says that you should always finish with your biggest blast. By going out with a bang, you leave a lasting impression that stays with the client long after your presentation is over.

Together, the doctrines of primacy and recency state that if you have a strong opening and a dynamite close, even if the stuff in the middle is somewhat mediocre you will still make a good impression.

Using this knowledge and the data from your Attention-O-Meter you would conclude that the very beginning and the very end of the session were the best times to communicate your most important information. And you'd be right. This is an opportunity for you to gain some real advantage.

## Opening the show

For clues and suggestions for making a strong opening go back to the research and brainstorming session you conducted and the themes you've determined to be important. Here are some samples of opening lines and themes you can use in a smack-me-between-the-eyes opening. When I say "opening line," that's exactly what I mean. Don't start with "Good morning" or "Thank you for inviting us here" or any other line that your competitor is sure to use. Head straight into the good stuff.

If the client's key hot button is:

**Schedule,** you might start with:

> *"This morning we are going to show you how your bridge reconstruction project can actually be completed in less time than you anticipated. We have analyzed the project in depth and we have discovered at least six areas where time can be saved. We are going to share these ideas with you today."*

**Technical issues**

> *"As you streamline and automate the city's water filtration and sewage disposal system, you have wisely chosen to integrate their control with the use of a SCADA system. In our meeting today, our chief programmer is going to review the system we intend to design for you to make sure you fully understand how the system will work, what safeguards are built in and how your operators will be trained in the use of the system. We will be illustrating our discussion with case studies from the SCADA systems we have designed and installed for Greenbury and Harpers Mills."*

**The approvals process**

> *"This project would be a piece of cake if it weren't for the challenge of gaining EPA approval. In our presentation this afternoon, we are going to focus almost exclusively on the process we will use to apply to and then negotiate with the EPA for your VIP (Very Important Permit)."*

**Construction costs**

> *"We are all aware of the instability of construction costs in this market. No one is more concerned about controlling them on your behalf than we at Smith & Jones. In our interview this morning, we will show you the many techniques we are going to use to ensure that, throughout the design and contract document process, construction costs are estimated and maintained as closely as possible."*

Compare any of these bold openings with the standard approach of "We are thrilled to be here presenting to you today. . . ." Any client, with those hot buttons front and center in their mind, will sit up and pay attention.

# Don't ever . . .

Your opening 60 seconds are like gold. Treat them carefully and extract the highest possible value from them. In order to preserve the high value of your opening minute, be sure you *never:*

- . . . open with a joke. You are a professional design firm, not stand-up comics. Although its perfectly all right and even desirable to incorporate a few chuckles into your presentation, most people are not naturally humorous and their jokes fall flat. Opening with a joke is not professional, it's old and corny.

- . . . start by giving a dictionary definition of a word or phrase. This has been done so often that it's almost as old and corny as starting with "Did you hear the one about . . ." People know what the words mean. They want to hear what you are going to do about their problem.

- . . . say "Thank you for the opportunity to present to you this morning." It sounds trite and insincere, and it's guaranteed to be what everyone else starts with.

- . . . apologize for anything. "I'm sorry we were a little late getting here." "I apologize for the poor quality of the overheads." "I'm sorry for the fact that [name of important firm representative] couldn't be here this morning." There are two lessons to be learned here. First, if you had done your planning and preparation and focused on the details you would have nothing to apologize for. Second, as soon as you point out something that is wrong, you give the client a great excuse for scratching you off the list of contenders.

- . . . use the first two minutes to cover administrative detail. You've got 60 seconds to grab their attention by the throat and put them on the edge of their seats. Reviewing the corporate structure of your Joint Venture or pointing out where the bathrooms are does not accomplish this goal.

- . . . think small. Instead think big. Big, bold thoughts stir the imagination and get your client thinking along with you. If you are truly to be thought of as the only firm to take on this project, you have to think, act and be bold.

## Keeping their attention

The attention level of an audience is high at the beginning and end of a session and low in the middle. Your job is to grab their attention early and keep it. Your first obligation is to address the client's question, "What's in it for me?" If you can't do that at the very beginning, you won't have their interest in the first place and you won't be able to regain what you never had.

Assuming you do capture their interest at the beginning, it's a real challenge to sustain that interest. Don't worry that they aren't hanging on your every word. The audience needs to take little mental breaks during the course of a presentation. Allow them to take these mental mini-vacations but give them a good reason to come back .

The average person's attention span is very short—a matter of a few minutes. Knowing this, you can plan to insert little "attention spikes" into your presentation. If you remember our imaginary Attention-O-Meter, the attention level dropped dramatically during the middle of the interview. By injecting an item of interest, telling a story or introducing a physical prop, you can reclaim the attention that you're losing. Attention spikes are verbal or visual devices that bring a group back together. For example:

*"In summary . . ."*

Don't wait until the end of the show. You can summarize as often as you like. Each time, you will get everyone's attention back because they don't want to miss the important point.

*"Now I'm going to show you . . ."*

Words like this indicate that something new is about to happen. The audience want to see if it has relevance for them, so they will tune back in while you introduce the new topic.

*"I know you'll appreciate this . . ."*

This speaks directly to your client's search for direct benefits. If you say they will appreciate something, they don't want to miss out.

*"Here's something you may not have known . . ."*

This appeals to the natural curiosity that is embedded in human nature. Everyone is bound to sit up and pay attention when you open a paragraph with this phrase.

*"Let's take a look at . . ."*

This brings you and the audience together in a joint activity. You are also giving the audience an instruction which they are happy to follow.

# 13

# Preparing Your Presentation

Before you begin getting ready for your presentation, ask yourself this question:

> *"If I can assume that they will leave this presentation remembering one thing and only one thing, what would I like that thing to be?"*

Because the truth is that that's all they will remember. At best they'll remember one thing that you said. And you need to figure out what that one thing needs to be. What is the story that needs to be told?

When you are getting ready for your presentation, don't begin by asking how many slides. Don't ask how many bullets per slide or what the background should be. Instead, start here:

**Wall of blank notes**

Literally, with a blank wall and blank Post-It notes. Whenever I am asked to help with a presentation or develop a "winning strategy," this is where I begin. And we start asking questions:

*'Tell me about this client."*

*'What's keeping him awake at night?'*

*'What motivates her?'*

*'What are the drivers on this project?*

Go back to your answers to the four questions you asked before you wrote the proposal (see Chapter 6). Go back, also, to the research you conducted in the go/no-go decision process (in Chapter 4). As you come up with answers to these questions, start to think about how you might address them.

You need a process to think, and to think freely, to capture any and all ideas, no matter how wild and crazy. You can capture these ideas on the Post-It notes and stick them on the wall. Then you can see similar, supplementary or related ideas. You can write more notes, stick them up, move them around, group them, rearrange them and modify them until it starts to look right and make sense as a compelling story.

Since this exercise is all about "How we're going to solve this problem for you," you need to have the entire project team (or at least the key players) involved in this brainstorming process. Sometimes you need a facilitator. That's where your marketing team or an outsider can play a role. You need someone who can help draw the ideas out of you and help you set aside the predictable ideas and go looking for the innovative and unusual.

You're so used to sitting down and saying things like "How many bullets, how many slides?" or "We need to have a slide on the history of the firm" or "Let's show them some projects we've done that are similar." If you start this way, you will already have fallen into a terrible rut of presenting in a certain manner and miss the fact that it's an ineffective way to communicate.

So I encourage you to start with this brainstorming approach and create a story board. You might be familiar with the concept of a storyboard. Movie makers use this tool to sketch out the elements and sequence of the story they are going to tell. They create some rough visuals that they intend to use to help tell the story. It's by no means the finished product, but it's a fast, flexible tool that can change easily.

©iStockphoto.com/evrenselbaris

**A storyboard**

As you brainstorm and build your storyboard, identify the key points that you have to get across. What is your main message? What are its main elements? Don't list a dozen points. At best you'll only be able to make *three*. More often than not, you'll only be able to make one. Go back to the start of this chapter and read that statement again. And again.

Then answer this question:

> *"Why should the client care?"*

When you get up to do your presentation, your clients have just sat through five other interviews, they are brain-dead and they're wondering, "Why on earth should I care about this?" as you drone on about more lists of projects you've done for other people. And all the client is doing while you're talking is doodling on a piece of paper because their brain has left the building.

Every point you make must have a direct and relevant importance to *this* client. If you can't be completely clear as to why the point is important, that's a good clue that you should simply skip over that point. It doesn't need to be made.

Don't forget: If you have 10 points that you want them to remember, they won't remember any of them. If you can get them to walk away with one dominant idea, then they will absolutely remember it.

Remember those themes that you identified way back in Chapter 6? This would be a good time to revisit them and see which ones are relevant to your presentation.

Let's go back and visit with that 48-year old state DOT employee from Chapter 6 again. If he's on the selection committee, perhaps what you want him to remember and take away the notion that "we are a safe choice." You want him to leave the interview knowing in the pit of his stomach that there is no risk to him by hiring you.

What about the case where you have a committee and everybody wants something different? If there is a clear leader, your primary theme should address his or her major concerns. But then you can talk about other things, too—all under the overarching theme that you've chosen. For example, let's say that your overall theme is the "safe choice" mentioned above. But you also have to address schedule. You would talk about the project schedule, but the emphasis of that discussion would be on how you've developed the schedule to produce a minimum of risk. You have established forced early deadlines and regular update meetings to ensure the schedule does not slip. All the while you are talking about schedule and other key points, you are reinforcing the theme of "safe choice" over and over.

Have you ever been involved with a project where the primary objective was not to widen a road or put in a new sewer line, but in fact was to get the mayor reelected? Sure, you've worked on that project or one very similar. In that situation and others like it, the main point that you want to get across is "We understand what the real objective is here."

Let's look at an example of how all this can come together in a presentation—how to focus on the specific issue, to take advantage of attention levels, to connect personally and to be memorable. That's a long list of things we're trying to do here but it's quite possible and can even be a bit of fun!

## The bats

A large A/E firm had been short-listed on a federal project worth over $100 million and I was asked to help choreograph the upcoming interview. The interview was restricted to just 45 minutes so we knew it was vital to make a lasting impact in the shortest possible time.

We had identified two major "hot buttons" on the project. The first was an environmental concern about an endangered bat species living in caves on the site. The bats would have to be protected both through construction and during the ongoing use of the facility.

The second issue was related to the choice of the site in a depressed, rural corner of one of the country's poorest regions. The federal government wanted the project to act as a stimulus to the local economy.

We knew about the concept of declining attention levels and we knew that we only had an opportunity to make a very small number of significant points. Using the two hot buttons as focal points, we crafted two separate, 20-minute, high impact presentations on these topics and walked into the interview, first team up at 9:00 AM.

We could have walked in and started by saying, "Good morning, we're from Acme Engineering, and we're pleased to have the opportunity to be here, blah, blah, blah..."

Then, once everyone had drifted off, we would talk about how we would address the issue of the bats. Here's what our PowerPoint slide might have looked like if we had taken that strategy.

**Endangered bat protection strategies**

•Restricted access to caves

•UVA science advisors

•Continuous monitoring of bat environment during construction phase

•Partnering with local schools for science learning opportunities

**Bat bullets**

We would have read the bullet points as the audience read along with us. They would have fallen asleep quickly and none of our content would have registered or been remembered. Classic cognitive overload.

Interestingly enough, the points on the slide do, in fact, represent the right technical approach. That is what needed to be done to protect the bats. We knew it and all our competitors knew it. And it's a pretty safe bet that the client was too intelligent to be influenced by the little piece of bat clip art on the slide.

Fortunately we didn't do take that road. We did something totally different.

At 9:00 our team walked in. They didn't say, "Good morning." They didn't say, "How do you do?" They didn't say, "Thank you for letting us be here today." Instead they said, "We're here to talk about the bats." And at 9 o'clock in the morning, on a screen that was about 8 feet tall, they flashed the following image:

**The bat**

Every single person on the selection committee gasped and nearly choked on their coffee. That is the absolute *last* thing they were expecting to see. Let's face it, that is one ugly critter. We said, "We'd like to introduce you to the bats. This is what one of them looks like. Perhaps you've never met one up close and personal!"

Now we had their attention. And their attention level was very high.

We had gone down into the caves and collected jars of bat dung (which has a special odor all its own) and we dumped it out on the table and told them, "This is what's in the bottom of the caves." Then, with this as a background, we told the story of how we were going to protect the bats and their environment. We never put up the slide with the bullet points, but we walked through the process while they looked at the bat face and smelled the bat dung as we passed around a second jar.

When the team had finished with the bats, everyone in the audience took a mental break as their attention level fell. Knowing they weren't listening too hard, we took this opportunity to cover the least interesting material and we introduced the members of the group and the key subconsultants.

Once that tedious ground was covered, we launched a second intense discussion about the economic development plan for the local area. With $100 million in construction at stake, we had invited the local economic development officer to participate and bring statements of support from local politicians. We talked about the contacts we had made with regional contractors and suppliers and the detailed plans we had for a local job fair prior to the start of the project. By the time we reached the climax of that story, the 45 minutes were up and we closed with audience attention at the highest possible level.

> **Moral:** It takes nerve to swim against the current, but the reward of a signed contract for the $100 million project made it worth every drop of sweat.

## Engaging multiple senses

One of the things that we did very consciously in the "bat" presentation was to engage multiple senses. In a typical presentation you involve sight and hearing. But the remaining three senses aren't activated. To the degree that you can involve more of the senses, you will be more memorable. And you can be sure that to this day, those people remember that presentation because it was so totally unexpected and because we engaged their sight, hearing, smell and touch. (We decided to pass on taste!)

You can do the same thing. What can you bring to your next presentation that you can pass around for the client to touch and hold? How about a jar of waste water? A brick sample? An old section of rusty pipe that you've dug up from a previous utility project? A soil sample? A concrete core? There are so many tangible "artifacts" from your work that you could bring to a presentation not only to engage an additional sense but to bring what you do closer to their experience and to make your presentation more memorable.

And when you bring that concrete core, drop it on the table so they actually experience the weight and sound of the concrete. When you pass the jar of wastewater around, invite them to take a sniff and take away the memory of the power of what you do when you transform that wastewater into clean water that can be safely put back into the river.

By engaging additional senses you drive home the points you are making, keep the audience involved and paying attention and increase the likelihood that they will not forget your presentation.

You should want, as much as possible, to be memorable. To the degree that you can engage taste, touch, and smell in addition to hearing and sight, then you can achieve your goal. Because bat dung is tactile, the clients would more likely remember the smell and the feel and the weight of the jar of dung they held in their hands. Now the client has a much more vivid sense of what you're going to do for them. They know how much the components weigh and they have a sense of how they fit together. And they start to remember.

Think about what happens when you go to an outdoor concert, when you're sitting outside under the stars, smelling the blossoms, feeling the breeze, hearing the music. That creates a memorable event that sticks in your mind forever. The more we can engage these senses, the more memorable your presentation becomes—which is why I like to bring stuff that they can touch and smell, and, once in a while, that they can taste. If the presentation is at 3:00 in the afternoon, I might bring chocolate chip cookies. "Here, it's mid-afternoon, we're all dragging our butts a little by now, have a cookie." I've even done presentations at 5:00 in the afternoon where I've brought beer.

But don't let me hear, "Hey, he said he brought beer and it worked. We should always bring beer!" Is that always appropriate? *No!* Absolutely not. But in that situation, with that client, at that time, it made sense and it worked.

I will also be the first to confess that I've had wild ideas and said, "Oh! Let's do this!" And then have it blow up in my face completely. But I'll also be the first to tell you that I would much rather go down in flames and come dead last because we tried something bold, than I would come second. Coming second is as easy as falling off a log. Coming first is hard. Coming dead last is also hard. But I'd rather come dead last than come second.

I believe that today, the riskiest thing that you can do is to play it safe and be normal and predictable and like everyone expects you to be. I think that's about the riskiest thing you can do because that's a guarantee that you'll come second.

Remember what I said in the introduction to this book: At all times remember that our objective is not to be cute or gimmicky. Our objective is enormously serious and our approach is based on the art of communication. How do I get an idea that's in my head successfully transferred to your head? We use these techniques, not because they are unusual or novel. We use them because they can more effectively communicate an idea.

# 14

# More Presentation War Stories

## The little firm that could

Remember back in Chapter 10 when you learned about the small firm in Greensboro that did the wild-and-crazy proposal with the food fight from *Animal House* because they had nothing to lose? Then you'll remember that, using that nothing-to-lose approach, they found themselves on a short list of 3 out of 49 firms that had submitted.

Faced with now having to make a presentation, the firm at first balked and thought to do a conservative, predictable PowerPoint show. Fortunately, they were able to see that they should continue to ride the horse that brought them that far, so we started brainstorming again. And this is a photograph of the actual presentation.

**Presentation to N.C. State University**

They walked in with two big cork bulletin boards, about 3' x 4'. At the start of the presentation, four black and white photos of the existing facility were already pinned to the boards, but nothing else. They had a bowl of push pins, a stack of Post-It notes and a collection of pictures and other "stuff."

They started by saying, "We're going to tell you how we're going to get this project completed successfully. First, we want to tell you who is here today." They then proceeded to rather forcefully pin each of the firm's logos onto the bulletin board. The "rather forcefully" part is because when you slam the pin into the corkboard you get a very satisfying "bang" and a very effective attention spike. People don't expect you to make a loud noise when you pin a scrap of paper to a bulletin board in a "professional" presentation, and so their level of intrigue is at the top.

So now they had the panel's attention and they proceeded to tell about the five components that would be necessary for success on this project. They had a scrap of paper ready and they slammed it onto the board as they said, "The first one is student involvement. These students are annoyed that the cost of this project is coming out of their pockets so we have to engage them as we design it and pay attention to the dollars that we're spending." They then pinned up an old wrapper from a Ramen Noodles package to let the panel know that they were sensitive to life on a student's budget. "And we have a cost consultant on board who is going to be keeping a tight fist on the money we're spending." As they pinned up a picture of a fist tightly squeezing a pile of dollars.

They talked about the Facebook page they were going to set up to encourage information sharing about the project and they stuck up a Post-It note about that. They talked about the "town hall" meetings they were going to conduct and they stuck up a note about that. At each turn they also referred to another project they'd done on which they'd used similar techniques and approaches, and they pinned up pictures of those projects.

Through the interview the two bulletin boards rapidly filled up with these notes, artifacts, pictures and ideas. Sustainability, innovation, scheduling, coordination—each of these topics was subject to repeated banging as pins and paper were stuck to the boards. John Belushi showed up a few times to reinforce the theme of the generational differences. And they ended up after 30 minutes by saying that they'd arrived at organized chaos—which pretty much describes a food center on a big university campus. You've got people eating, you've got people sleeping. Some are Facebooking on their cell phones and laptops and that's what this project is going to be all about.

"But," they said, "we can't have organized chaos on the project. We've got to really organize it and be in charge of keeping everything moving forward in a predictable manner. And here's how we're going to stay on top."

At that point they took a ball of red yarn. They said, "We're going to start right here with student involvement," and they wrapped one end of the yarn around the pin through that piece of paper. "Then we're going to address sustainability and move on to innovation." As they mentioned each of the five critical points, they literally wrapped the yarn around the project and tied it into one nice neat bundle.

The end of this story is that the little firm that "didn't stand a chance" beat out 47 other firms in competing for this project. The sad news is that they had to beat out 48, but they made a significant impact on the client and definitely got on their radar screen for the next project. They are sure to be invited back for involvement in future projects.

How did this particular presentation come to be? Why did they choose to do it that way? Because they sat down and asked themselves about the client. They analyzed what was going on in the heads of the selection committee members. They did not do it to be gimmicky, cute or clever, but to communicate an idea. And they brainstormed to determine the best way to communicate that idea, to those people, at that time. The best way to communicate a different idea to different people at a different time is likely to be an entirely different approach. That's why you should always start with the storyboard. And why you should *never* start with "Click here to add title." Always start by identifying the story that needs to be told. Then you'll discover the best way to tell that story.

> **Moral:** If 'bold' works when you've got nothing to lose, it's even more effective when you're in the lead.

# Slam dunk on a white board

The architect was a small firm in a western state. They had asked me if I could help them prepare for an upcoming interview for which they had been short-listed. I changed my travel plans and arrived in their office at about 8:00 on a Saturday morning, the week prior to Christmas.

The interview was set up for Tuesday morning and the client was coming to the architect's office. The firm's two principals, the project manager, and I met in their boardroom to discuss our strategy.

I first asked them what they had already planned for the session. At that point they were going to give the client a brief history of the firm, a short slide show of recent projects they had completed, and an introduction of the project team. They had also planned to surprise the client with a perspective sketch they had prepared of a design idea for the project.

At this point, I asked the architects to stop for a moment and switch hats. I asked them to pretend they were the client with all his worries and concerns and then to tell me about the project. It took them a moment to get into the "role playing" mode, but I soon heard an interesting story.

The client was a small developer who had inherited some land from his family. Every year he would sever a small parcel off the main property and develop a small commercial project. The current project was a speculative office building of about 20,000 square feet.

The developer had already retained an architect who had produced a design and some construction estimates. Based on these, the client went looking for building tenants before he actually spent his construction dollars. And boy, did he find a tenant! The U.S. Forest Service signed a 10-year lease for the entire building. The developer was in heaven — this was a tenant who would take the entire property, pay their rent every month, and not kick holes in the walls. For a landlord, it doesn't get much better.

Then he got the phone call. The architect he had retained—a one-man operation—had suffered a heart attack and was in the hospital. While the prognosis was good for recovery, he was in no shape to work on the project. The developer had a signed lease with a move-in date but was getting no closer to having a building. He was sweating bullets!

Now he was desperate to find a replacement architect who could get the client moved in on time.

Having heard this fascinating story, I didn't bother to point out to my client that not one thing they were planning to say in their interview would address the obvious question that the developer had front and center in his mind: "Can you get it done in time?"

At this point I asked the partners if they thought they could meet the tight schedule. They replied that they could. When I asked, "How?" they replied that they intended to put their best team on it. I told them that trite rhetoric about "best teams" was as meaningful as motherhood and apple pie. What were they *actually* going to do in order to meet the deadline?

At this point the architects started getting specific. Since the board room had very large whiteboards on two walls, I asked the project manager to grab a marker and start taking notes.

First, they concluded that, if the interview were on Tuesday, they would need a decision by Wednesday afternoon at the latest so they could get going. Next, they started to list key decisions that would have to be made and assigned dates to them. They listed contractors and suppliers they would contact to arrange and long-lead materials or equipment that was needed. They decided that, since the Forest Service had already been a client of their own firm and they knew the staff, they could work directly with them for tenant fit-up work. That would save at least three weeks over working through the developer.

As the architects brainstormed about their actions, the project manager took notes on the board. One board listed nothing but critical meeting and milestone dates. We went on like this for three hours, by which time two full walls of whiteboard were full of notes. Most importantly, they had concluded that they could get the project done about three weeks ahead of schedule.

By this time it was noon. The architects and the project manager looked at the notes and said it was great that we had worked out the schedule, but "When were we going to start working on the presentation?" I replied, "We're done! It's the Saturday before Christmas, I'm going to catch an early flight and get home." The look of shock on their faces told me I would have to explain a little more.

"Look," I said, "your developer is lying awake nights, frantic that he won't be able to meet his obligation to the best tenant he's ever had. He already knows you can design the project, that's why you're on the short list. The only thing he wants to know is whether you can get it done on time or not. You've just proven you can, so what else is there to present?"

This approach was new to them so they asked, "Shouldn't we be making some boards or slides or something?"

"Look at that whiteboard," I instructed. We've just spent three hours of hard work figuring out a solution to his problem. There was sweat dripping from the board! "No," I said, "we're going to walk out now and go to lunch, then I'm going home and you won't come back in here until Tuesday morning when you will go over these notes and show him how the project will be done." I then went a step further and told them, "If you do it like this, I guarantee that you will win this project." Although a little nervous about this outside-the-box tactic, they agreed. "Call me on Wednesday to let me know how it went," I called as I headed for the airport.

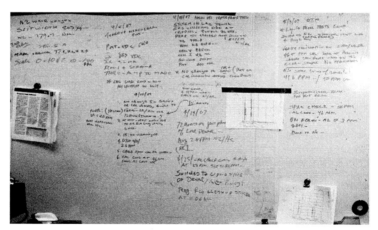

**The white board**

The next Wednesday they called as expected. They could hardly contain themselves as they related what had happened.

The developer arrived and sat down in the boardroom. As they started going through the notes on the board, he madly took notes and asked questions. Once, when they pointed out a crucial meeting date, the developer held up his hand and said, "I think I've got a conflict on that date. Would it hurt us to move the meeting back by one day?"

When a client makes a statement like that in an interview, you know and I know that the firm already has the project.

When they were finished, he handed them the project on the spot and offered them a fee that was about 20 percent higher than they had intended to ask for. Then he sat for the next half hour and ridiculed the other firms he had interviewed. "These people," he said, "sat there and talked about the history of their firm, showed me slides of projects they'd done, and introduced the team to me. But you showed me how we could get it done!"

Finally, on his way out the door, the client turned to the partners and said, "I do three or four projects like this every year. I get the feeling that we might be able to work well together!"

> **Moral:** Nothing is more important than what is going on in your client's head.

## So what?

The A/E firm had asked me to conduct a training seminar in delivering presentations, so we had spent the better part of the day as a video camera recorded design professionals laboring through the slides, boards and scripts of their most recent interviews. Without fail, each time someone got up to speak, they turned their back on the audience and watched as slide after slide of past projects was shot onto the screen.

I patiently reminded them that they needed to let the audience know why they should look at a particular slide and what benefit they could expect to gain from that knowledge. But as the afternoon wore on, it was obvious that I wasn't getting through.

In desperation I pulled out a big fat marker and wrote "So What?" on a piece of paper. Every time someone would say, "And here's another project we've done," I would hold up the sign and force them to explain the relevance of the project they were showing on screen to the one at hand. It was a painful process and I wasn't sure the lesson was really sinking in. So we decided to raise the stakes.

The firm had a project interview coming up the following week and I made them a dare. I dared them to invite the client selection panel to use the "So What?" signs.

The firm was in the mood for risk-taking and they agreed to try it. We used the laser printer to prepare some professional-looking signs and mounted them on popsicle-stick handles. (How professional can a sign that says "So What?" be?)

As the presentation team was introducing themselves at the interview the following week, they handed one sign to each member of the review panel. They instructed that members that, if at any time during the interview they felt their time was being wasted or the team was talking about things that didn't seem relevant to them, they were to hold up their signs.

The client thought this was a little odd, but the novelty intrigued them and they had sat through too many lifeless interviews to object.

It wasn't long before the old habits started to surface. One of the presenters slipped comfortably into his old routine of showing off his slide collection with his back to the audience. But this time, someone held up their "So What?" sign.

When that happened, the presenter stopped, thanked the client for helping him improve the quality of his presentation, and pointed out that a particular technology used in the project shown in the slide was going to be used to solve a very similar problem on the current project. A couple of questions followed, along with a chuckle.

From that point on the interview was completely changed. Every time someone put up a "So What?" sign—which quickly become a fun game for the client—not only did everyone have a good laugh, what could have been a stuffy monologue became a high-energy dialogue. There was an electric exchange of ideas and the client and the firm kicked off a dynamite relationship.

When the interview was over, the firm was handed the project on the spot. In the client's words, "Any firm who has the nerve to come in here with signs like this is the kind of firm we want to work with." But they had one condition: they wanted to keep the "So What?" signs because, again in their words, "We attend plenty of meetings where these signs would be invaluable!"

When you're standing up there, why is "So What?" such an important question? It's because the client is saying, "Hey, you're here to serve me. You're here to solve my problems on my project. And all you're doing so far is telling me about someone else's problem. I don't care about somebody else's problem. I want to know about how you're going to solve my problem."

**Moral:** "What's in it for me?" is the client's favorite question.

# 15

# The Center of the Universe

Throughout this book I've repeated again and again that nothing matters except what your client wants. I've spoken about how everyone shares the same favorite subject—themselves. And how you must always build your entire sales effort by first crawling inside your client's head to see what the world looks like from that vantage point.

So it makes sense that we allow your clients to have the last word in this book. Over the years I've collected comments from your clients. They come from formal debriefings, comments made during interviews and casual conversations. They provide invaluable insight into what goes on in those important heads. So pay attention.

**1. This is the text from a memo sent by the marketing director of a construction firm following their team's loss on an interview.**

*Re: Recent presentation.*

*Comments from client:*

- *No one showed enthusiasm.*
- *I understand that superintendents and field staff might not be the best speakers, but the rest of the team showed no enthusiasm at all.*
- *It really affects how we react to you.*

*Prior to the presentation, we were all in the room getting ready and waiting for the client to arrive. The client's Head of Facilities walked in and our guys were so focused on what they were going to say, that they never even got up to say "Hello."*

*We lost.*

**2. This is the text of a memo from a business development representative of an engineering firm.** The firm was getting ready for an upcoming interview and the BD rep was relating a (rare and valuable) conversation he'd just had with the head of the selection committee. (Names have been changed.)

*Hello folks,*

*I wanted to pass onto you all a conservation I had with Susan Lee today. Susan is the Director of the Engineering Department and on the selection committee. I was advised not to ask her about the project from someone close to her, but I had to call her regarding a grant we were helping the city and a local non-profit with. At the end of the conservation she asked me if there was any information I needed for the Flood Study. Well, I was prepared and below are my notes verbatim.*

1. *"All the remaining firms are strong technically. They are all about equal so what it will come down to is who are the folks that are really excited about the project, who really want to do the work, and who do we (being the city) feel we will be able to work with the best."*

2. *When asked if she likes one central presenter or the entire team, she responded with the following: what makes our team strong is the team itself. Therefore she personally would like to hear from the different team members but mentioned that we should not have any team members present who are "overbearing" or that are strong technically but will not connect with the selection committee. If any of the speakers are "technically dry" do not have them present.*

3. *Also make sure the team is well organized so the transitions between speakers are smooth and fluid. Avoid distractions during the transitions. All speakers need to stay on point and connect with the committee.*

*So it seems that we will want to work towards making a strong connection with them, be enthusiastic with good energy, and have all the speakers make sure that they are not "technically dry." Basically we want them to like us.*

*Thanks and I hope this is helpful.*

*Bill*

**3. This is an evaluation checklist used by a client organization when reviewing submittals and interviews by consultants.** It asks two very pertinent questions that your business development effort must answer. At the end of the day, when your proposal has been read and you've completed your presentation, how would your client answer these questions?

> 1. *When reading about how the firm is going to handle our current project, are we acutely aware of the benefits this firm will bring us? Is it apparent this firm is different from all the others we've reviewed? Is their approach to solving our problem clear and sensible? Are we left with a high level of confidence this firm can handle the project without any difficulty?*
>
> 2. *When learning about the project team and its individual members, do we feel we are getting to know them personally? Are we convinced they can do the job? Do they seem like the sort of people we would want to work with on all of our projects? Are we anxious to work with them?*

**4. The last item is a memo that was written more than 25 years ago.** The author was a principal in a design firm who had just "sat on the other side of the table." In other words, he had just experienced what it's like to be a client to whom design firms are trying to sell services.

Although the memo is written in the context of an interview, these thoughts apply throughout the entire business development cycle. His advice and encouragement to the other members of his firm is as applicable today as it was then. It's as good and on-target as it gets.

> *I spent all day yesterday listening to four joint venture firms give presentations for their services. It drilled home once again that good business development is essential if we are to sell work. In the Olympics there might be 18 inches difference between first and last place runners—and all the losers could easily win races elsewhere.*
>
> *We are up against increasingly stiff competition. We're competing against people who really understand good marketing techniques, good sales, and good presentations. We've got to be outstanding to close that last 18 inches.*
>
> *Here are some thoughts that occurred to me yesterday. We've discussed them all in the past, but I wanted to re-emphasize them to you.*

1. *Make sure we understand what the client wants.*

   *You can't find that just by reading the RFP. You've got to talk to the people who are doing the hiring. Those people are usually available. I was surprised yesterday at how few people talked to me or the other members of the interview committee before the interview. We were all available for questions.*

2. *Include the buyer benefits.*

   *Most of the presenters told us what they were going to do. But they didn't emphasize what the benefit to us would be. Sometimes we were able to infer the benefit; sometimes we couldn't. A few of the better presenters described their services in simple, declarative sentences, and then explained the benefits that would accrue to us if we hired them to provide those services.*

3. *Prepare and rehearse.*

   *It was clear that some of the firms had spent time preparing for us, and some of them had not. The ones that prepared were well organized. They addressed important points with simple, declarative sentences, and they seemed relaxed and unconfused. The ones that hadn't prepared and rehearsed stumbled all over themselves, corrected one another and missed the mark.*

4. *Don't talk about yourself too much.*

   *Several of the companies failed miserably because they just told us all about themselves and what they had done. We'd already read all about that in their proposals. What we wanted to know was how they were going to do our job. The companies that came out on top were the ones that spent all their time talking about how they were going to do things for us.*

5. *Excitement and innovation sure help.*

   *The firms that came out on top were those that clearly were excited by the opportunity, and had innovative approaches. It was clear who had thought the job through and who came in with their canned "we're big and this is the way we do it" approach. The companies that sold their traditional services failed. Those that met the unique needs of the project succeeded.*

There you have it: An entire book summed up beautifully in just five points by someone other than the author. I couldn't have said it better myself.

Now it's your turn to get out there and knock 'em dead!